NEIGHBOURHOOD

SALADS, SWEETS AND STORIES FROM HOME AND ABROAD

HETTY MCKINNON

Photography by Luisa Brimble

plum. Pan Macmillan Australia

For Ross, Scout, Dash and Huck ~ for being the people I like to feed the most xx

CONTENTS

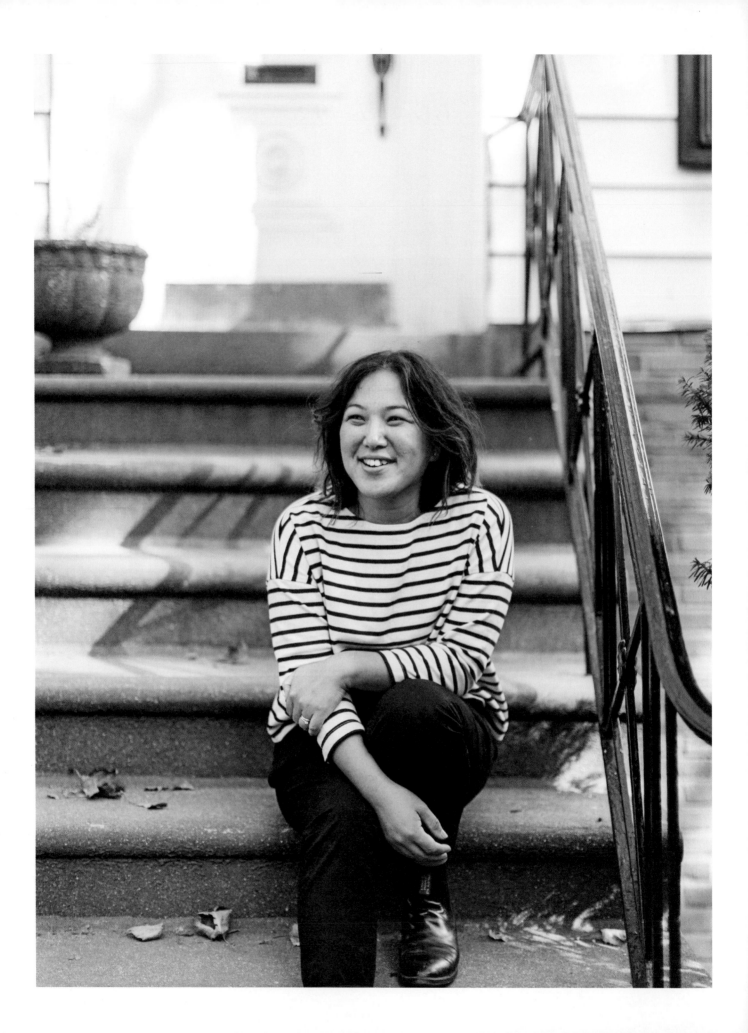

COMMUNITY *AND BEYOND...*

Since the release of my first cookbook in 2013, my community has become infinitely larger. This book has taken me outside of my Surry Hills community and into the kitchens of countless cooks from all corners of the globe. Imagine my thrill when I stumbled into a gorgeous cafe called Maison Bastille in Paris to find *Community* sitting proudly on the shelf. My little book has been fearlessly flying the salad flag a long way from home.

The '*Community* juggernaut', as I've come to call it, has been incredibly overwhelming and still continues to grow. Over the years, I have received countless messages of support from readers telling me about their personal experience of *Community*. What I think people take away from *Community* is that you don't have to be a vegetarian to enjoy vegetables, and you don't have to be a chef to be a good cook. Interestingly, I have witnessed a movement that is about so much more than food; it is about the importance of feeling connected with others. It is a timely reminder that, even amongst the hustle of our modern lives, simple acts like cooking for others, eating together and sharing food still resonate strongly.

Two years on, my life has taken a few twists and turns. In late 2014, my husband and I packed up our home on Arthur Street, bid adieu to Surry Hills and headed north. We landed in France and ate our way through the local Provençal markets. We introduced our children to the sights, sounds and tastes of Italy, Germany, Finland and our old 'hometown' of London. Finally, we ended our trip in Brooklyn, New York, where the next chapter of our lives and Arthur Street Kitchen begins.

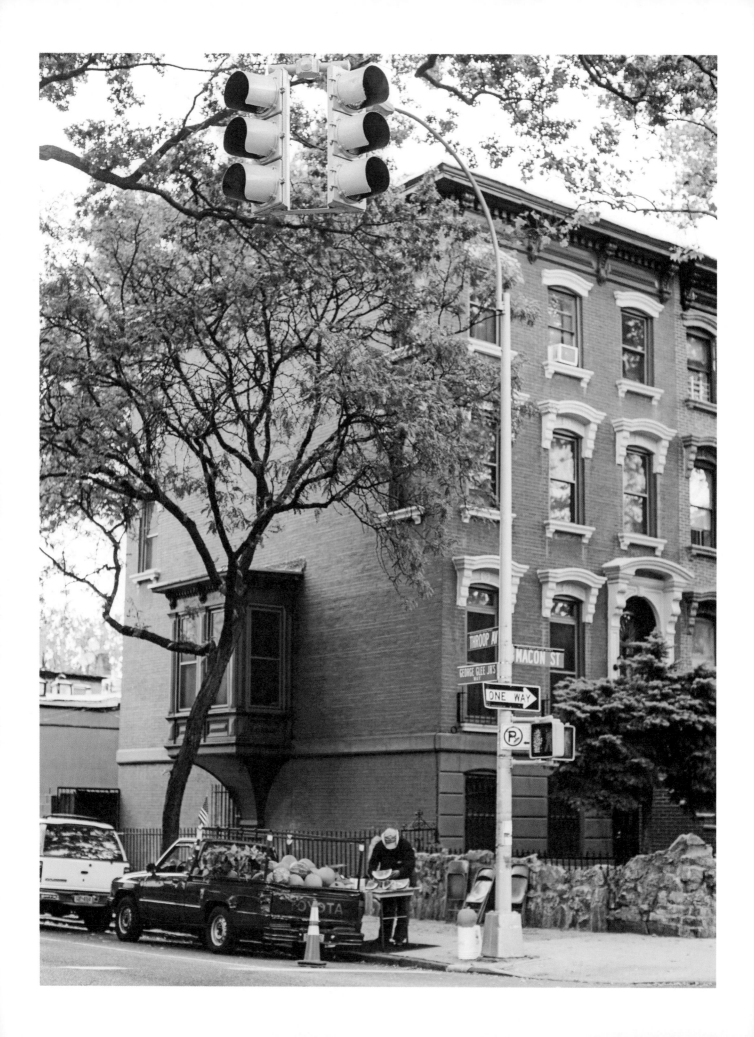

FROM COMMUNITY *TO* NEIGHBOURHOOD

This book takes its cues from *Community* and ventures a little bit further. *Neighbourhood* is a collection of salad and sweet recipes inspired by 'places', journeying from Brooklyn in New York to the greater Americas, the Mediterranean, Asia, France, my native Australia and many other places around the world for salad-making inspiration.

If community is a feeling of kinship, *Neighbourhood* is a physical compilation of the sights, sounds and colours of a geographic area. Growing up in Australia, and having lived in London, travelling extensively through Europe, before settling in brownstone Brooklyn, I have been continually drawn to the role of food as a social anchor in a neighbourhood. No matter where you live in the world, it is the daily rituals of food that strongly influence the way we live. It is the places we visit daily – whether it's grabbing a cream cheese bagel from our corner bodega, picking up fresh mozzarella from the local deli, or buying seasonal produce from the Greenmarket – that have inspired my latest salad-making adventures, with exciting new international flavours and bold new vegetable pairings.

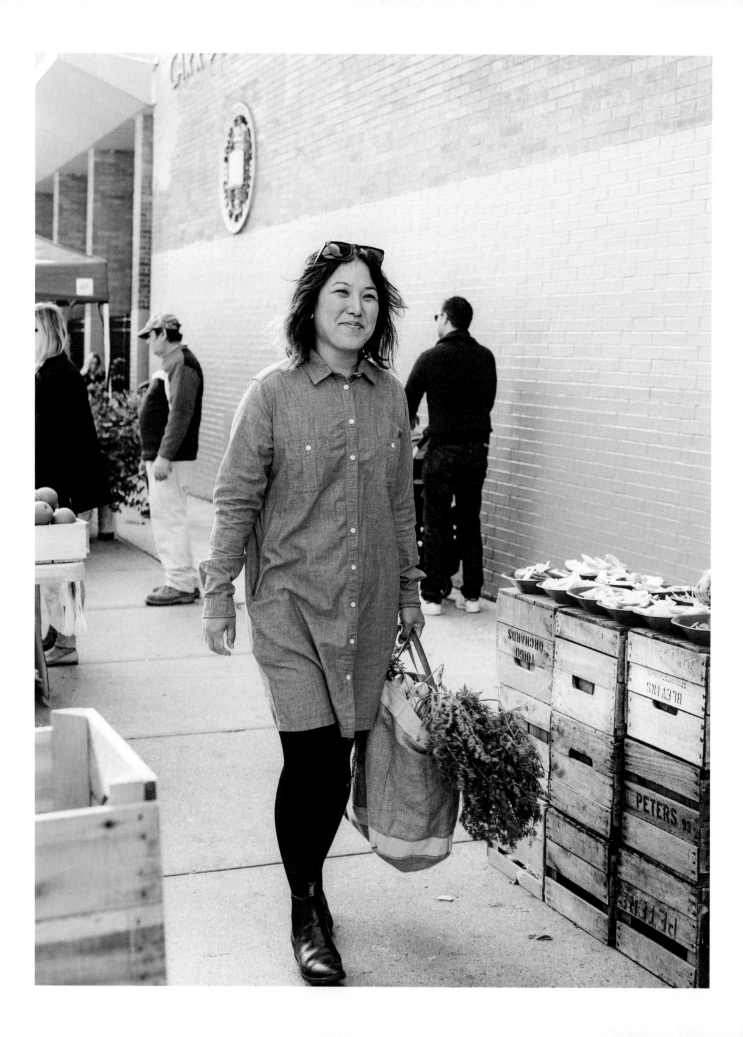

THE NEIGHBOURHOOD

It can be said that New York City is a city of neighbourhoods. Each has their own unique personality, forged from history and circumstance. Often, entire neighbourhoods are founded on the culture of food. From the Chinatowns of Lower Manhattan, Sunset Park in Brooklyn and Flushing in Queens, to Koreatown around 32nd Street, the Little Italies in Manhattan and Bensonhurst in Brooklyn, the curry and spice emporiums of Murray Hill, the colourful Indian and Pakistani food in Jackson Heights, the old-world Russian delicacies in Brighton Beach, and Greek and Egyptian treats in Astoria, culinary neighbourhoods like these are the beating heart of New York City.

When we put down roots in Carroll Gardens, a charismatic neighbourhood of deep-fronted brownstones and a robust Italo–American background in south Brooklyn, I was struck by the strength of history in the area. Over the last few decades, Carroll Gardens, like many Brooklyn neighbourhoods, has undergone a cultural makeover. With that, many of the old local haunts have closed their doors or moved deeper into the suburbs. But still, amidst the urban evolution, there remains a strong sense of neighbourhood in the area. Italian flags fly alongside American ones, ubiquitous Virgin Mary statues adorn front and back yards, while old-school delicatessens, pizzerias and enotecas still stand amongst the slick new wine bars and sleekly designed restaurants. This is an area with a strong narrative and a tenacious sense of its past, present and future.

A fundamental part of this neighbourhood story is in the local food. My local Italian deli, Caputo's Fine Foods, has been a neighbourhood institution for over four decades, a family-owned store where the owner makes fresh mozzarella (several times a day!), and supplies fresh and dried pasta, antipasti, olive oils and more. Up the street, an unrelated bakery that happens to share the same name, Caputo's Bake Shop, has been supplying the neighbourhood with baked goods since the early 1900s. The ciabatta, especially the olive encrusted one, is my essential daily bread and their pizza dough is a family staple. Unassuming brick-fronted pizzerias owned by long-time locals still serve up crispy based, cheesy topped pizza pies to residents, old and new. On Sundays, the Carroll Gardens Greenmarket thrills me with the colour of seasonal produce grown at farms nearby; most weeks, I still discover a fruit or vegetable that is unfamiliar to me. And in between, daily visits to my favourite local bodega, Sue's Organics, bring me reliably sourced produce and lively conversation.

In making Brooklyn home, it has been these humble, everyday neighbourhood haunts that have given me a tangible sense of belonging and connection. Through the hunting and gathering of food, I am gradually becoming a local.

NEIGHBOURHOOD

21

NEIGHBOURHOOD

If I had my choice, I would always advocate slow cooking. For me, one of life's great luxuries is to take the time to shop for the freshest ingredients, cook real food from scratch and share meals with family, friends and neighbours. However, I also appreciate that weeknight meals are often about being quick and easy. One of the most common questions I am asked is advice on how to make a salad quickly. My best advice on speedy salad making: GET PREPARED!

Here I've thrown together a few practical ideas on how to make your weeknight salad prep a bit easier and quicker.

ON THE WEEKEND, STOCK YOUR PANTRY

Let's be honest, having a thoughtfully stocked pantry is your first step to simplifying your weekly cooking. My confession here is that I'm a food hoarder. I love buying food items, even if I'm not in immediate need. You just never know, right? My friends used to joke that if we were faced with war and famine, they would bunker down at my house because my food stocks would keep us fed for months. But in my madness, there is some method. Getting into the habit of picking up a few essentials on a weekly basis will allow you to gradually build up your pantry stocks, inevitably making last minute cooking a whole lot easier.

On the weekends (or whenever you do your major household shop), stock up on basics you will need for the week. Here are some tips on how to stock your pantry, fridge and freezer for quicker and easier salad making:

Choose two or three main seasonal vegetables for the week
Picking up many different types of vegetables can make weekday cooking confusing. Instead, just pick two or three vegetables that are in season, inexpensive and look delicious. These vegetables can be the centrepiece of your meal, so instead of buying one cauliflower, buy two or three of them.

Pick two types of soft herbs to see you through the week
My favourites to have in the fridge are parsley, coriander, mint and Chinese shallots (see note page 32). These herbs are very flexible, can be used in a range of dishes and will really transform your salads.

Stock up on canned legumes
Great choices are chickpeas, borlotti beans, butterbeans, black beans and cannellini beans. If you have a can of beans, a vegetable and herbs, you virtually have a salad right there!

Make grains pantry staples

Stored in airtight jars, they keep for months and they are great to add bulk to your dish. I always have quinoa, pearl barley and bulgur wheat (cracked wheat) in my pantry as I find them so versatile and, importantly, quick to cook!

Stock your freezer with a few essentials

My freezer essentials are edamame beans, garden peas and lotus root.

CHOP IT UP

If you have a spare half hour on the weekend, chop up your veggies, ready for cooking. If you have kale, remove the stems and tear up the leaves. For vegetables like cauliflower or broccoli, cut them into florets and keep the stalks separate. Store everything in airtight plastic containers or zip lock bags and keep in the vegetable drawer of your refrigerator to keep crisp. This small step will make weekday cooking so much quicker. (Note: this only applies to vegetables that won't oxidise and turn brown when cooked, so a definite no to vegetables like potato, eggplant and artichokes.)

ROAST IN ADVANCE

Roast, barbecue, grill or pan-fry your vegetables in advance and keep them in the refrigerator. Most vegetables, without sauce or flavour added, will keep in an airtight container in the refrigerator for 1–2 days.

MAKE TOASTED NUTS AND SEEDS A PANTRY STAPLE

Toast a variety of nuts and seeds in bulk and keep them in airtight jars in your pantry. I usually have jars of toasted walnuts, almonds, peanuts, pistachios and sesame seeds ready in my pantry.

PRE-COOK A GRAIN

Consider cooking one or two grains in advance and keeping them in the refrigerator, ready for salad assembly. Quinoa keeps well in the fridge for 5–6 days, and can even be frozen for up to 6 months. Other grains that you could cook in advance are pearl barley, spelt, farro, freekeh and brown rice.

FRIDGE AND FREEZER DRESSINGS

Dressings can be made in advance, and either stored in the refrigerator or freezer. Vinaigrettes, flavoured yoghurts, or versatile Asian-style dressings are fine to store in the fridge for 2–3 days. Pesto and scented oils can be frozen for up to 3 months. Just make sure to bring the dressings back to room temperature before using.

FOUR WAYS TO USE LEFTOVER SALAD

In my house, there is often a plethora of leftover salad. The Chinese in me always has me cooking for the masses. So over the years, I have devised a few interesting, delicious ways to use up leftover salad. I thought I'd share these with you.

1. PUT AN EGG ON IT

When in doubt, put a fried egg on it.

Sometimes, if the salad is robust enough to do so, I like to quickly fry the leftovers in a little extra-virgin olive oil, just to add some heat, then top the whole thing off with a fried egg. Just like that, you have a hearty lunch or light dinner.

---

2. BLEND IT INTO A SOUP

I love blending leftover salad, transforming it into a hearty soup.

Simply throw your leftover salad into a food processor or blender, add a cup of vegetable broth or liquid vegetable stock and blend the whole mix up. This salad do-over is perfect for those salads without too many leaves and which are heavy with legumes or roasted vegetables. If you have a lot of leftovers, you can even freeze the soup for later consumption.

---

3. MAKE A CHEESE GRILL

A cheese grill is the perfect anytime and every time meal. Making a grilled cheese sandwich is serious business – especially in the United States where there is great pride taken in a perfect cheese grill. Use a sandwich grill if you have one, but here, I show you how to make the perfect grilled cheese sandwich using your everyday frying pan:

Take two thick slices of sourdough bread or ciabatta.

Spread butter on both sides of both slices of bread (yes, both!).

Layer one side of both slices with whole egg mayonnaise.

Heat a large non-stick frying pan or griddle pan over a medium–low heat and add the bread slices (mayonnaise-side down) to cook. Slide them around the pan to achieve an even golden colour.

Flip them both over, then pile one slice with leftover salad, and top with your favourite melty cheese – try cheddar, Swiss, gruyere, mozzarella, provolone, brie – and place the other slice of bread on the top, browned-side down (you want the uncooked sides on the outside). »

Cook the sandwich, moving it around the pan to get an even browning, for about 2 minutes on each side.

A grilled cheese sandwich is fantastic made with roasted broccoli, cauliflower, carrots, sweet potato and, my favourite, brussels sprouts.

---

4. GO KUKU!

Turning a salad into a kuku is perhaps my very favourite way of embracing leftovers.

Kuku is a rather exotic name for an Iranian-inspired frittata, laced with a subtle hit of saffron, and perfect served at room temperature. Over the years, I have made this dish countless times using leftover salads – it is great with roasted vegetable salads, but also works wonderfully with legumes and grain salads with bulgur wheat, spelt and barley.

SERVES 4~6

3 tablespoons extra-virgin olive oil
2 onions, halved and finely sliced
1 garlic clove, finely chopped
6 eggs
2 tablespoons plain flour
1 teaspoon baking powder
small pinch of saffron threads, soaked in 1 tablespoon boiling water
4 cups leftover salad
3 tablespoons chopped soft herbs (parsley, dill, mint, coriander, chives etc.)
½ pomegranate, seeds extracted
sea salt and black pepper

Preheat the oven to 180°C. Line a 22 cm springform tin with baking paper.

In a large frying pan, heat the olive oil and fry the onions and garlic for 7–8 minutes, or until the onions are soft and starting to caramelise. Allow to cool.

In a mixing bowl, add the eggs and whisk until smooth. Add the flour, baking powder, saffron and its soaking water, sea salt and a good grind of black pepper and whisk until smooth.

In the springform tin, lay out the onions, then spoon over the leftover salad. Pour over the egg mixture. Place the pan on a large baking tray (to catch any leaks) and bake in the oven for 45–50 minutes until golden and the egg is set. Insert a skewer to make sure the kuku is cooked all the way through.

To serve, scatter over the soft herbs and pomegranate seeds. Serve warm, or at room temperature. The kuku will keep in the refrigerator for 2–3 days.

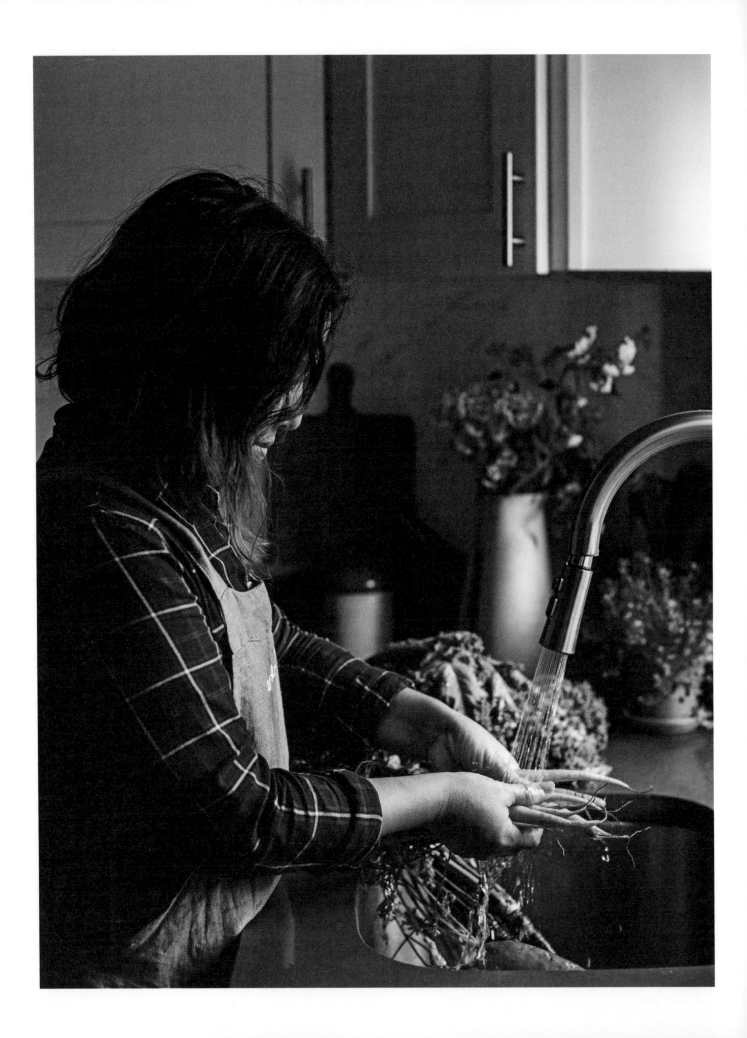

COOK YOUR BEANS WITH SALT AND GARLIC!

Like most people, as a young cook, I was taught never to add salt to the cooking water for legumes, lest we end up with hard skinned, inedible beans. But one day, I decided to experiment – I added a big pinch of salt at the beginning of cooking my beans, along with a clove of peeled garlic. The result? I have never looked back!

I have found that salting the bean cooking water helps them cook faster, adds so much flavour, makes the beans taste creamier and helps them stay much more intact! The truth is, beans are fairly tempestuous beings. You do need to play around with cooking methods and times to get things right. But I encourage you to persist because the results are truly worth it. In truth, many varieties of beans like borlotti, black eye, cannellini, and butterbeans don't take that long to cook – about 40–45 minutes from scratch. Chickpeas take a little longer, about 1 hour (depending on how fresh the dried chickpeas are – older chickpeas take a long time to cook and sometimes never soften fully). I don't even bother to soak them overnight, but soaking does speed up the cooking time.

How to: Cover your beans in plenty of water. Bring to the boil, and allow to cook on high heat for about 5 minutes. Turn the heat down to a low simmer, add two or three big pinches of sea salt and one clove of garlic. Cook until the beans are tender. At the end of cooking, the garlic should either be disintegrated, or will break up with a little stirring. Drain.

COOK YOUR GRAINS IN FLAVOUR

Making a salad is about building layers of subtle flavours. At every opportunity, I inject flavour into each ingredient of the salad. So when cooking grains like pearl barley, spelt, farro, freekeh, quinoa or rice, using vegetable stock, or well salted water will add so much more flavour to the final dish.

ALLOW GRAINS TO SIT AND FLUFF UP

After cooking grains like quinoa, bulgur wheat (cracked wheat) and couscous, give them 10 minutes or so to sit and 'dry out' slightly. I like to turn the stovetop off and leave the pot on the hot element to just allow the residual steam to evaporate naturally. This will leave you with fluffier grains.

ALWAYS EAT SALADS AT ROOM TEMPERATURE

If I was to give lessons about how to eat a salad, this would be my number one piece of advice – eat your salad at room temperature. With the exception of chilled dishes like soba noodles, I recommend eating all salads at room temperature to experience optimum flavour.

THE GOOD OIL

Unless otherwise specified, when I refer to oil, I'm talking about extra-virgin olive oil. In most cases, I use extra-virgin olive oil for the cooking of vegetables, along with dressings. This is purely out of convenience, as I don't often have many different types of oil in the kitchen. For me, extra-virgin olive oil is perfect on most foods! If you prefer a lighter oil, you can use standard olive oil or even a neutral oil like grapeseed.

For ease and clarity, I indicate how much olive oil will be required for a particular recipe. But I encourage you to use your own discretion. Some people love their food drenched in olive oil, and if this is the case, please do so! If you are cutting back on oily food, then use less. This is your call.

THE ONION ISSUE

A spring onion is a shallot is an eschalot! No, they are NOT all the same thing. To further complicate the issue, they are known by different names all around Australia. In this cookbook, for the sake of clarity, the image opposite shows you precisely what I am referring to when I use the terms Chinese shallot, spring onion and eschalot.

RECIPE NOTES

Cups and spoons of herbs and greens (like rocket, spinach, kale etc.) are always TIGHTLY PACKED.

I always use Maldon sea salt flakes.

For parsley, I only use the flat-leaf (continental) variety.

Black pepper is better freshly ground.

Be liberal and flexible with quantities, especially with your vegetables. As this is salad making and not baking, exact, precise quantities and measurements are not essential. So don't fret over the size of your cauliflower or sweet potato. Think about how many people you are cooking for and adjust the recipe accordingly! Leftovers are perfect for lunch the next day, sharing with friends and neighbours or perhaps trying my leftover salad ideas on page 26.

I've included symbols for dishes that are gluten free (GF) and vegan (VG).

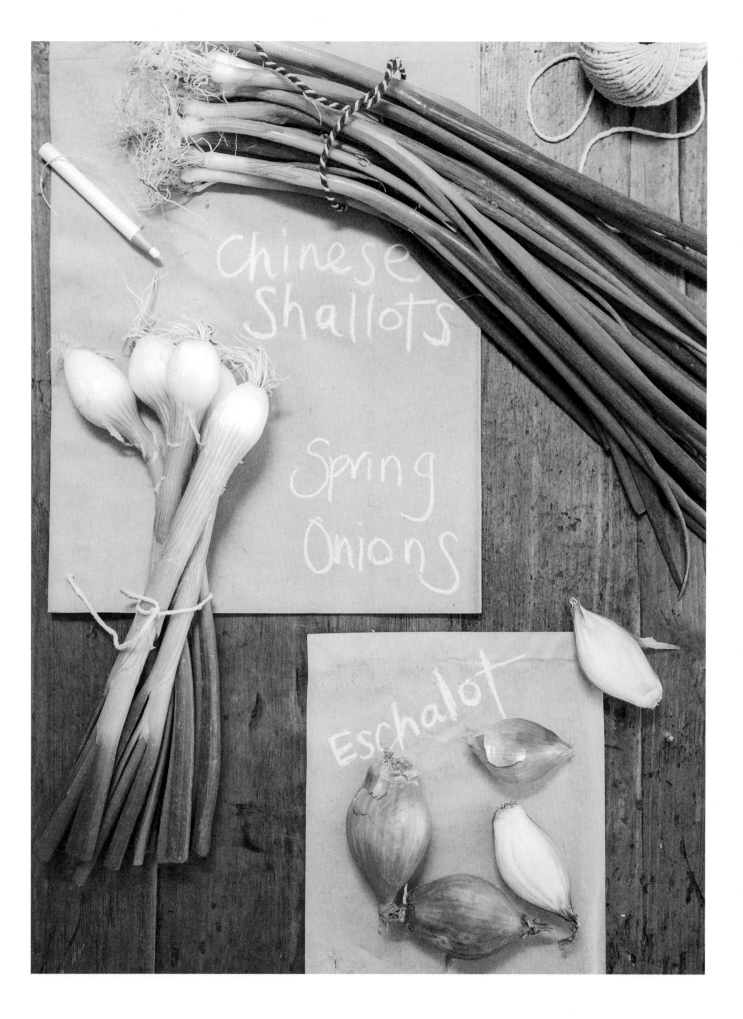

Chinese Shallots

Spring Onions

Eschalot

DEAR AMERICA,

Like the country and its people, the food in America is vast, diverse, passionate and bold. As I find my culinary feet in my adopted home neighbourhood of Brooklyn, it has been wonderful to meet the comforting flavours from the South, to be swept along with the lively Mexican wave and to embrace the fusion flavours of Latin cuisine. To live in New York City is to truly have the world's food at your front door, at whatever time of the day! Here, food fads are born and disseminated across the globe. Food is theatre, a full-bodied experience designed to entertain and challenge all your senses.

SHREDDED COLLARD GREENS, BAKED SWEET POTATO AND PINTO BEANS WITH PAPRIKA–BUTTERMILK DRESSING

Collard greens, with their deep green, thick leaves, stand up to lengthy cooking times, while still retaining their flavour and texture. For me, however, I also love them raw. For this salad, I'm celebrating the Southern roots of collard greens by teaming them with roast sweet potato, pinto beans and a spicy buttermilk dressing. I've written this recipe with substitutions for both collard greens and pinto beans, both of which can be hard to find outside of the United States.

GF | SERVES 4~6

3 sweet potatoes (about 700 g),
  unpeeled and cut into 1 cm cubes
3–4 tablespoons extra-virgin olive oil
1 bunch of collard greens (about 400 g),
  washed and stems removed
500 g cooked pinto beans
  (about 2 cans), drained
⅓ cup coriander leaves
½ cup sunflower seeds, toasted
1 lime, cut into wedges
sea salt and black pepper

PAPRIKA-BUTTERMILK DRESSING

185 ml (¾ cup) buttermilk
3 tablespoons sour cream
1 garlic clove, very finely chopped
1 teaspoon paprika
½ teaspoon smoked paprika
juice of ½ lime
1 tablespoon extra-virgin olive oil
sea salt and black pepper

SUBSTITUTES

collard greens: cavolo nero, kale
pinto beans: red kidney beans,
  borlotti beans

Preheat the oven to 200°C.

Place the sweet potato pieces on a large baking tray, toss them in 2 tablespoons of olive oil and season with salt and pepper. Roast for 20–25 minutes until tender.

Slice the collard green leaves very finely using a sharp knife and place them in a large bowl. Drizzle over 1–2 tablespoons of olive oil, add a pinch of salt and massage the oil into the leaves for about a minute (this will start to soften the leaves).

To make the buttermilk dressing, mix together the buttermilk and sour cream in a bowl and stir in the chopped garlic, paprika, lime juice and olive oil. Season with salt and pepper.

Combine the massaged leaves with the sweet potato, beans, coriander and sunflower seeds. Season again with salt and pepper, spoon over the buttermilk dressing and serve with the lime wedges on the side.

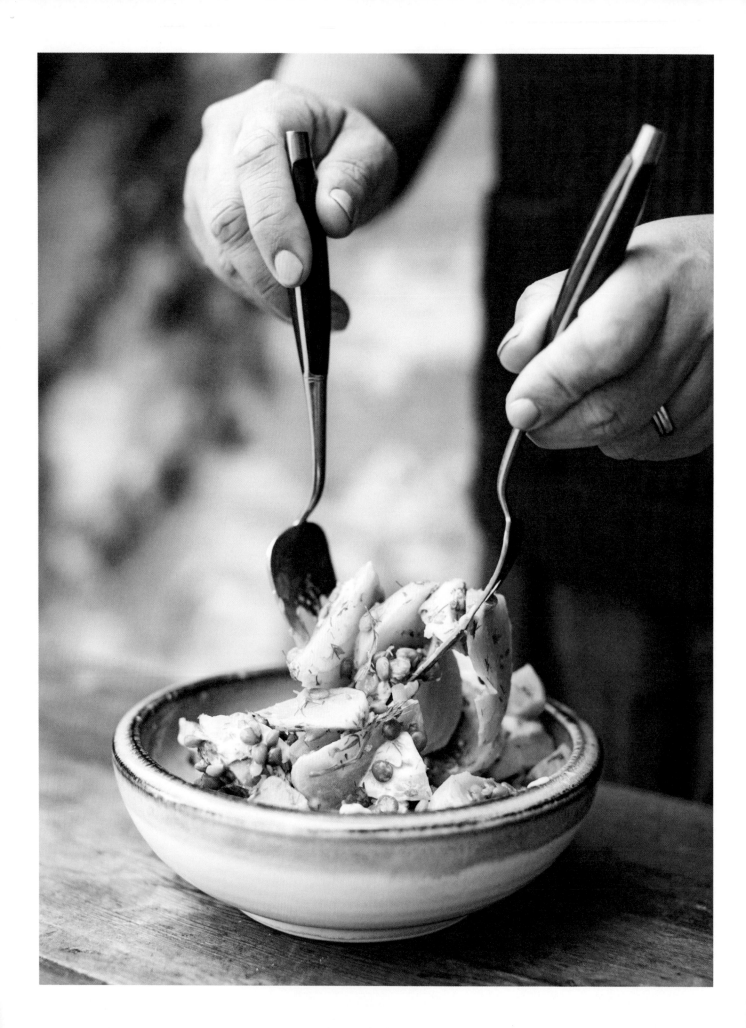

ROASTED GOLD BEETROOT WITH LENTILS, SOFT HERBS AND LEMON–SAFFRON YOGHURT

While gold beetroot are often near impossible to find in some parts of the world, they are excitingly abundant during the New York summer. Slightly less earthy and mellower than their crimson-hued equals, gold beetroot are like a ray of sunshine. This salad is exactly that – sunshine on a plate. Gold beetroot is enlivened with a bounty of fresh herbs and a sunny lemon and saffron yoghurt.

GF | SERVES 4~6

8 gold beetroot (about 1.6 kg),
   peeled and cut into 1 cm cubes
3–4 tablespoons extra-virgin olive oil
1 tablespoon white balsamic vinegar
400 g brown lentils, rinsed
2 cups soft herb leaves (parsley, dill,
   coriander, chives, mint, oregano
   or tarragon)
sea salt and black pepper

LEMON–SAFFRON YOGHURT

pinch of saffron strands
375 g (1½ cups) Greek yoghurt
2 tablespoons extra-virgin olive oil
squeeze of lemon juice
sea salt and black pepper

SUBSTITUTES

gold beetroot: red or target beetroot

Preheat the oven to 200°C.

Place the beetroot on a large baking tray, drizzle over 2–3 tablespoons of olive oil and the white balsamic vinegar. Season well with salt and pepper and roast for 30–35 minutes, or until the beetroot are tender.

Place the lentils in a saucepan and cover with plenty of cold water. Add a big pinch of salt. Bring to the boil, reduce to a simmer and cook for 20–25 minutes or until just tender. Drain.

To make the lemon–saffron yoghurt, place the saffron strands in a small bowl and pour over 2 tablespoons of boiling water. Allow to steep for 10 minutes. When ready, add the yoghurt to the saffron and water and stir to combine. Add the olive oil, squeeze in the lemon juice and season well with salt and pepper.

To serve, combine the beetroot with the lentils and all the herbs. Fold the yoghurt through, season with salt and pepper and finish with a drizzle of olive oil.

Dear America,

CHIMICHURRI SALAD BOWL WITH EGGPLANT, TOFU, FENNEL AND SHIITAKE MUSHROOMS

There is a lot to admire about chimichurri, an Argentinean paste traditionally used as a rub for meats. It is fiery, herby, tangy and garlicky, and offers a vibrant tang that is also perfect for marinating vegetables. Make it a day ahead to allow the flavours to develop even further. Here, I've taken chimichurri on an Asian journey, using it as a marinade for eggplant, tofu and fresh shiitake mushrooms. The yoghurt tames the spice. The chimichurri can be made 24 hours ahead and, if you want to get extra prepared, it is also okay to marinate the vegetables in the chimichurri overnight.

GF | SERVES 4~6

2 eggplants (about 800 g)
1 fennel bulb, shaved
400 g firm tofu, cut into 1 cm cubes
200 g fresh shiitake mushrooms (or other
   Asian mushroom such as oyster),
   cleaned and trimmed
185 g (¾ cup) Greek yoghurt
550 g cooked brown rice
1–2 tablespoons extra-virgin olive oil
½ cup coriander leaves
3 tablespoons white sesame seeds, toasted
sea salt and black pepper

CHIMICHURRI (MAKES 250 ML/1 CUP)

2 garlic cloves, very finely chopped
2 teaspoons sea salt
½–1 jalapeño chilli
1 teaspoon paprika
1 teaspoon ground cumin
80 ml (⅓ cup) red wine vinegar
1 cup flat-leaf parsley leaves, finely chopped
2 tablespoons oregano leaves
2 tablespoons chopped Chinese shallots
   (see note page 32)
250 ml (1 cup) extra-virgin olive oil

SUBSTITUTES/OPTIONS

eggplant/mushroom/fennel: zucchini,
   carrots, sweet potato, asparagus
For vegans, omit yoghurt

To make the chimichurri, place all the ingredients in the bowl of a food processor and whizz it all up. It is up to you how much jalapeño chilli you use – I suggest starting with a small portion and adding more as you go along. Alternatively, use a mortar and pestle to grind everything together. Leave to sit for at least 30 minutes, or for up to 24 hours.

Peel strips of skin from the eggplants, from top to bottom, so it leaves a stripy pattern. Cut the flesh into 1 cm cubes. Place the eggplant, fennel, tofu and mushrooms in four separate bowls. Spoon about 1 tablespoon of chimichurri over each, toss to coat, transfer to the refrigerator and leave to marinate for at least 30 minutes, ideally overnight.

When ready to cook, heat a large frying pan or griddle pan over a medium heat. Working in batches to avoid overcrowding the pan, fry the eggplant cubes until golden and tender. Remove and allow them to rest in a colander. In the same pan, cook the tofu until golden. Finally, fry the mushrooms until cooked and golden.

To serve, place a dollop of yoghurt in the centre of a large serving bowl and arrange the eggplant, tofu, mushrooms, brown rice and raw marinated fennel around it. Spoon over any remaining chimichurri, season with salt and pepper, drizzle with the olive oil and scatter over the coriander leaves and sesame seeds.

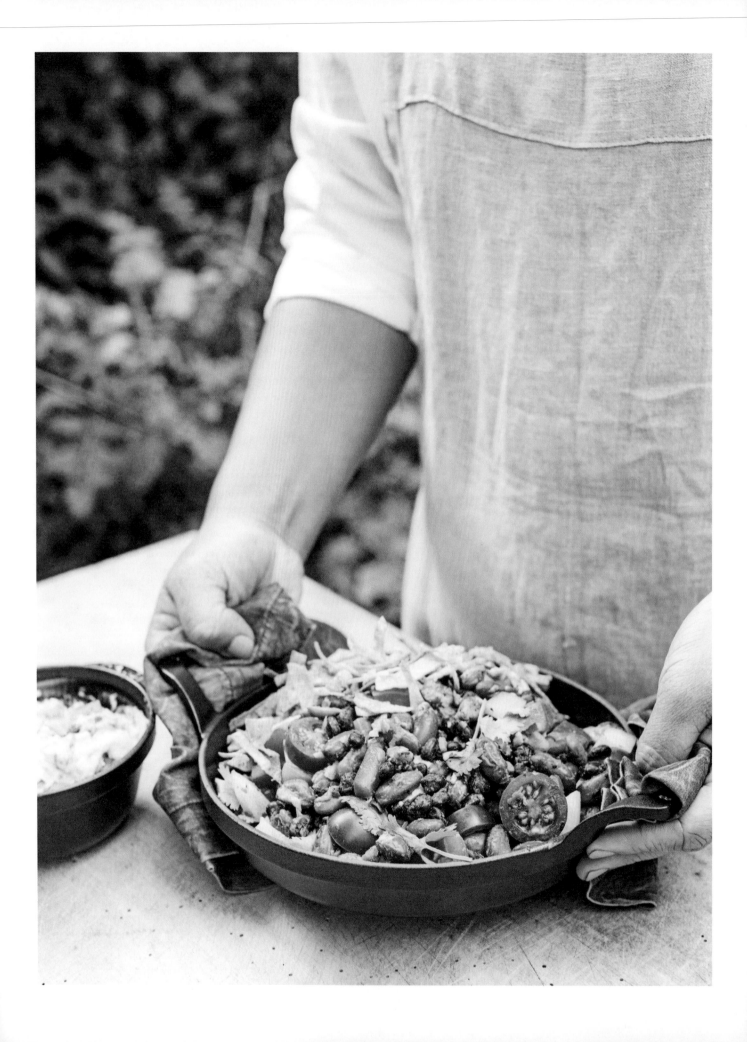

BEAN CHILLI WITH CRISPY TORTILLA STRIPS AND CREAMY AVOCADO SALSA

Before we arrived in the United States, I didn't quite grasp the pervasive, powerful influence of Mexican-inspired food here. Like in Britain where you 'go out for a curry', chilli comes close to being the national dish in America. While not necessarily traditional or authentic, chilli is actually a blend of Mexican and southern American influences that has worked its way into most local kitchens. In our Brooklyn home, chilli is our winter Sunday evening staple, ceremoniously and meticulously prepared by my husband Ross.

GF | SERVES 4~6

3–4 tablespoons extra-virgin olive oil

1 onion, finely diced

1 garlic clove, very finely chopped

2 teaspoons cumin seeds

2 teaspoons paprika

2 teaspoons chipotle powder

2 teaspoons dried oregano

500 g cooked pinto beans (about 2 cans)

500 g cooked black beans (about 2 cans)

500 g cooked red kidney beans (about 2 cans)

200 g cherry tomatoes, halved

2 capsicums (red, yellow or 1 of each), deseeded and cut into 1 cm dice

1 cup coriander leaves

1 lime, cut into 6 wedges

sea salt and black pepper

CRISPY TORTILLA STRIPS

6 corn tortillas

1–2 tablespoons sunflower oil

pinch of sea salt

small pinch of chipotle powder, mixed with a pinch of paprika powder

CREAMY AVOCADO SALSA

2 large avocados (about 600 g), diced

1 tomato, deseeded and finely diced

1 eschalot (see note page 32), very finely diced

1 Lebanese cucumber, deseeded and finely diced

1 long red chilli, deseeded and finely chopped

3 tablespoons natural yoghurt

juice of 1–2 limes

2 tablespoons extra-virgin olive oil

sea salt

Preheat the oven to 200°C.

Heat 2 tablespoons of olive oil in a large frying pan over a medium heat, add the onion and garlic and cook for 5 minutes or so, until soft. Add the cumin seeds, paprika, chipotle powder and oregano and cook for 30 seconds, until fragrant. Drain the beans and add to the pan, drizzle with some more olive oil, season well with salt and pepper and fry the beans for 6–8 minutes, until they are just starting to get crispy. Remove from the heat and leave to cool completely.

For the crispy tortilla strips, brush each side of the corn tortillas with sunflower oil and stack them on top of each other. Cut them in half, then slice each half into 6 mm strips. Spread them out in a single layer on a large baking tray, sprinkle over the salt and the chipotle and paprika spice mix and toss gently. Bake for 10–15 minutes, or until crispy.

To make the avocado salsa, put all the ingredients in a bowl and stir to combine. Season with salt, taste and add extra lime juice if necessary.

To put the salad together, combine the beans with the cherry tomatoes and capsicum in a large serving bowl. Drizzle over some olive oil, top with the crispy tortilla strips and coriander and serve with the avocado salsa and lime wedges on the side.

CHIPOTLE BLACK BEANS WITH COLLARD GREENS, AVOCADO AND CHIPOTLE–LIME VINAIGRETTE

When I arrive in a new place, one of the first things I do is explore the local supermarket. I love seeing the foreign packaging, the familiar and unfamiliar brands and discovering new produce. For me, the supermarket shelf is a snapshot of a neighbourhood's food culture, habits and rituals. In our early days in Brooklyn, we stayed temporarily in Williamsburg, where the local supermarket shelves were lined with countless chipotle chilli products. This dish is an ode to chipotle and my other great American love, collard greens. This salad is smokin' hot.

VG | GF | SERVES 4~6

2–3 tablespoons extra-virgin olive oil
1 garlic clove, very finely chopped
½ red onion, finely diced
1 dried chipotle chilli, soaked in boiling
   water for 30 minutes, drained and
   finely chopped
500 g cooked black beans
   (about 2 cans), drained
1 bunch of collard greens (about 400 g),
   stems removed and very finely sliced
2 large avocados (about 600 g), diced
½ cup pumpkin seeds, toasted
½ cup coriander leaves
sea salt and black pepper

CHIPOTLE–LIME VINAIGRETTE

1 dried chipotle chilli, soaked in boiling
   water for 30 minutes, drained and
   finely chopped
juice of 1–2 limes
125 ml (½ cup) extra-virgin olive oil
1 teaspoon ground cumin
1 teaspoon caster sugar
1 garlic clove, very finely chopped
sea salt and black pepper

SUBSTITUTES

black beans: red kidney beans
collard greens: cavolo nero, kale

Heat the olive oil in a large frying pan over a medium heat. Add the garlic, onion and chipotle chilli and cook for 2 minutes, then add the black beans, along with a big pinch of salt and toss well. Continue to cook for 3–4 minutes until the beans are slightly crispy.

To make the chipotle–lime vinaigrette, add the chopped chipotle chilli to a bowl with most of the lime juice, olive oil, cumin, sugar and garlic. Whisk together, adjusting the lime juice until you achieve your preferred acidity. Season with salt and pepper to taste.

Combine the black beans, collard greens and avocado. Spoon over the chipotle–lime vinaigrette, season well with salt and pepper and toss everything together. To serve, scatter over the pumpkin seeds and coriander leaves.

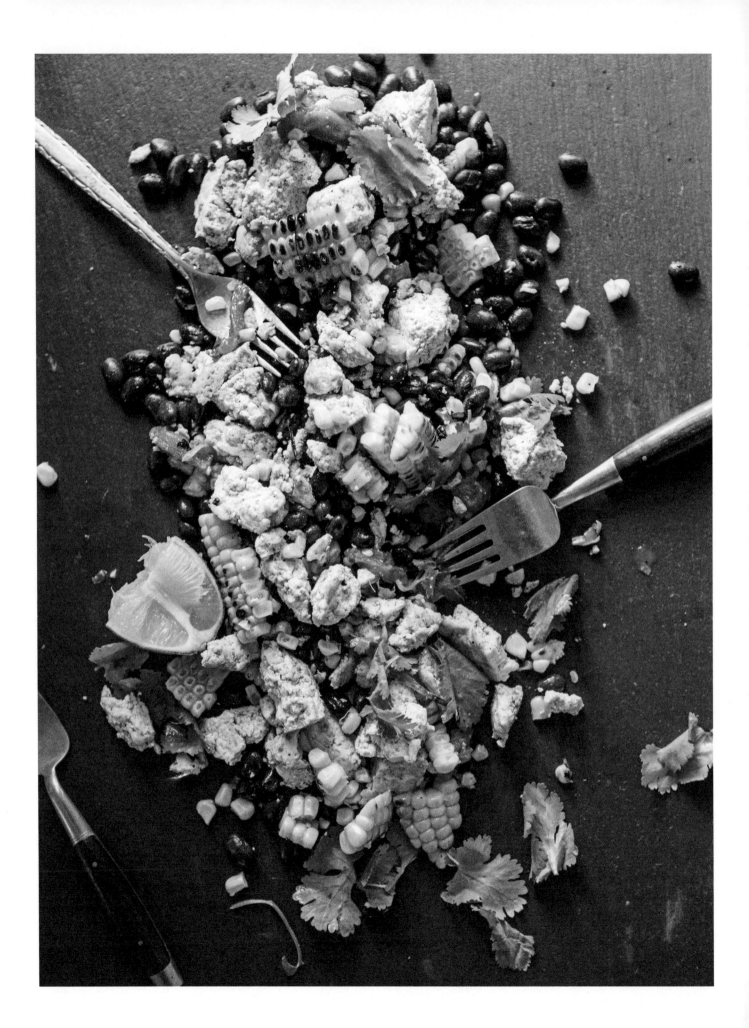

SPICED TOFU WITH BLACK BEANS, BARBECUED CORN AND RED CAPSICUM

This recipe is one of many twists and turns. It started off as a scrambled tofu stir-fry, inspired by a Sophie Dahl recipe. But, as with many dishes in my repertoire, it soon morphed into a salad of Tex Mex influence. The heavily spiced, smoky tofu is really one of my favourite things to eat. My kids love it just as much. Roll up in a corn tortilla or soft taco shell for a simple, flavour-packed family meal.

VG | GF | SERVES 4~6

2 red capsicums (about 350 g)
3 corn cobs (about 550 g)
2–3 tablespoons extra-virgin olive oil
2 eschalots (see note page 32), peeled and finely diced
1 garlic clove, crushed
800 g firm tofu, torn into chunks
½ jalapeño chilli, deseeded and finely diced
2 teaspoons ground cumin
½ teaspoon ground turmeric
1 teaspoon smoked paprika
500 g cooked black beans (about 2 cans), drained
½ cup coriander leaves
juice of 1 lime
sea salt and black pepper

SUBSTITUTE

red capsicums: store-bought chargrilled capsicums

Preheat a griddle pan or barbecue. You need it smoking hot.

Lay the capsicums on the pan or barbecue and cook for 10–12 minutes, turning, until blackened on all sides. Place the capsicums in a bowl, cover with plastic wrap and leave to steam for 10 minutes. When ready, peel off and discard the charred skin along with the seeds and membrane and roughly chop the capsicum flesh. (To save on time and effort, you can definitely use store-bought chargrilled capsicums.)

Add the corn cobs to the pan or barbecue and cook on all sides, until slightly charred. Leave them to cool slightly, then run a sharp knife down each side to remove the kernels.

In a large frying pan, add 1–2 tablespoons of olive oil and the eschalots and garlic and cook over a medium heat until the eschalots are translucent. Add the tofu chunks, then the chilli, cumin, turmeric and paprika and move around, making sure the tofu is evenly coated in the spices. Add a big pinch of salt and pepper and cook for 5–6 minutes until the tofu is starting to take on some golden colour.

Combine the capsicum, corn, black beans, tofu mixture and coriander and mix well. To serve, squeeze over the lime juice and finish with a drizzle of olive oil.

MUSHROOMS AND KASHA
WITH RAINBOW CHARD AND RADISH

Kasha is another name for roasted buckwheat and it is very popular in Russia and Ukraine where it is one of the oldest known dishes in Central and Eastern European cuisine. I hadn't eaten much kasha over the years, but recently in Little Ukraine in New York City's East Village, I experienced the loveliness of kasha and mushrooms stuffed in cabbage. The dish was so wonderful it got me thinking about the possibilities of kasha and mushrooms as a new salad power couple. Say hi to my 'KashRoom' salad. Stay alert when you are cooking kasha as it will quickly turn to mush if you overcook it. The trick is to add the stock a little at a time and taste often to see when the grains are just ready.

GF | SERVES 4~6

400 g kasha (roasted buckwheat)
3–4 tablespoons extra-virgin olive oil
1 litre (4 cups) vegetable stock
1 garlic clove, very finely chopped
400 g mixed mushrooms
    (any variety), cleaned
300 g rainbow chard with stalks,
    finely sliced
20 g butter
1 cup soft herb leaves (mint,
    coriander, parsley or chives)
4 radishes (about 150 g), trimmed
    and very finely sliced
juice of ½ lemon
sea salt and black pepper

SUBSTITUTES/OPTIONS

kasha: pearl barley, quinoa
rainbow chard: Swiss chard,
    silverbeet, spinach
For vegans, omit butter

Coat the kasha grains in 1 tablespoon of olive oil and a few big pinches of salt. Mix together well to coat the grains evenly.

In a large shallow frying pan, add the kasha and cook for 20 seconds over a medium heat. Then add a little stock, stir and leave to simmer on a medium–low heat. When the liquid has been absorbed, add enough stock to cover the kasha grains and continue like this until the kasha has softened enough to eat, but is still a little crunchy. Don't let it cook too long as it will turn to mush. Place the kasha into a bowl.

In the same frying pan, add 1 tablespoon of olive oil and the garlic and cook over a medium–high heat for 30 seconds. Add the mushrooms, season with salt and pepper and cook until all the mushroom juices have evaporated. Add a further 1 tablespoon of olive oil along with the chard stalks and cook for 60 seconds. Finally, add the chard leaves and cook for another 30 seconds or so, just long enough to wilt the leaves. Take off the heat and add the butter to the mushrooms and chard, leaving it to melt through the mixture.

Combine the kasha with the mushrooms, chard, herbs and radishes. To serve, squeeze over the lemon juice, drizzle with olive oil and season with a little salt and pepper.

BRUSSELS SPROUT CAESAR WITH CROUTONS, BORLOTTI BEANS AND SUNFLOWER SEEDS

The caesar salad is very much the perfect Italian–American invention. Nowadays, every self-respecting salad-maker needs to have a caesar recipe in their repertoire. This one is mine. This caesar shamelessly delivers flavour while also offering a nutritional punch – there are raw brussels sprouts from the antioxidant-rich brassica family, teamed with health-kicking borlotti beans and vitamin E-packed sunflower seeds.

SERVES 4~6

250 g stale bread, torn into 2 cm chunks
1–2 tablespoons extra-virgin olive oil
500 g brussels sprouts, trimmed
500 g cooked borlotti beans
  (about 2 cans), drained
½ small red onion, very finely sliced
½ cup flat-leaf parsley leaves, chopped
½ cup basil leaves, roughly torn
½ cup sunflower seeds, toasted
60 g parmesan, shaved
sea salt and black pepper

CAESAR DRESSING

6 garlic cloves, unpeeled, plus ½ garlic
  clove, very finely chopped (optional)
250 g (1 cup) whole egg mayonnaise
80 g (⅓ cup) sour cream
1 tablespoon salted capers, rinsed
  and chopped
juice of ½ lemon
sea salt and black pepper

SUBSTITUTES

brussels sprouts: kale
borlotti beans: chickpeas, cannellini
  beans or any other canned legume

Preheat the oven to 200°C.

Coat the bread in the olive oil and sprinkle with salt. Spread over a large baking tray in a single layer and bake in the oven until golden, about 15–20 minutes, turning every now and then to make sure the croutons are evenly browned and crisp on all sides. Cool.

While the croutons are baking, make the caesar dressing. Place the unpeeled garlic cloves in the oven and cook for 20–25 minutes until they are very soft. Remove from the oven and peel off the skins, then mash the soft garlic flesh with the back of a fork and mix it together with the mayonnaise, sour cream, capers, lemon juice and 3–4 teaspoons of water. Season to taste with salt and pepper and – if you like it more garlicky – add half a very finely chopped raw garlic clove.

Using a mandoline or the grater attachment on the food processor, very finely slice the brussels sprouts.

Combine the brussels sprouts with the borlotti beans, red onion, herbs and half the sunflower seeds. Add the caesar dressing, season with salt and pepper and mix everything well to make sure the ingredients are well coated. Leave the salad to sit for 15–20 minutes to allow the brussels sprouts to soften and the flavours to meld together. To serve, fold through the croutons and sprinkle over the parmesan shavings and remaining sunflower seeds.

SUGAR SNAP PEAS WITH RADISH AND SPELT GRAINS

When I met natural foods chef, food writer, blogger and native New Yorker Jodi Moreno, I knew I had found a friend. Jodi and I share a lot in common, including a love of vegetables and grains. One fine spring day, Jodi brought a bag of sugar snap peas to my Carroll Gardens apartment and prompted me to eat them raw, sliced in razor thin strips. What a revelation! This is the surprising, nourishing grain salad that I shared with Jodi, brought to life by these juicy, crunchy sugar snaps.

SERVES 4~6

400 g spelt grains
400 g sugar snap peas, trimmed
4 radishes (about 150 g), trimmed
4 Chinese shallots (see note page 32),
  finely chopped
½ cup coriander leaves
2 tablespoons sesame seeds
sea salt and black pepper

GINGER, HONEY AND LEMON DRESSING

2.5 cm piece of ginger, peeled and grated
1 small garlic clove, grated
juice of 1 small lemon
2 tablespoons honey
1 tablespoon sesame oil
80 ml (⅓ cup) extra-virgin olive oil
sea salt and black pepper

SUBSTITUTES/OPTIONS

spelt: pearl barley, farro, freekeh
sugar snap peas: snow peas, asparagus
For gluten free, use quinoa in place of spelt
For vegans, use maple syrup in place
  of honey

Add the spelt grains to a saucepan of salted water and bring to the boil. Reduce the heat and simmer, uncovered, for 30–35 minutes until the grains are tender. Drain.

To make the dressing, combine all the ingredients in a small bowl and whisk together. Season well with salt and pepper.

Using a sharp knife, finely slice the sugar snap peas lengthways. Shave or slice the radishes into thin rounds. Place the sugar snap peas and radishes in a large serving bowl and add the shallots, coriander leaves and spelt grains. Add the ginger, honey and lemon dressing, season with salt and pepper and toss to combine. To serve, scatter over the sesame seeds.

FREEKEH WITH DELI VEGETABLES, KALE PESTO AND CHILLI–PARMESAN SUNFLOWER SEEDS

This salad is an homage to all the multi-cultural delicatessens that are the heart of so many neighbourhoods around the world. Invariably family run, the local 'deli' is your go-to, where you can reliably find a great selection of cheeses, cold meats, pasta, olive oils and marinated vegetables. This salad uses your favourite deli ingredients – try deliciously wilted Moroccan olives, perfectly acidic artichoke hearts, stunningly shrivelled sun-dried tomatoes, smoky chargrilled eggplant or juicy salted capers. The addition of kale pesto and chilli–parmesan sunflower seeds elevates this throw-together salad from simple to spectacular.

SERVES 4~6

4 cups marinated deli vegetables (about 2 kg)
  such as sun-dried tomatoes, artichokes,
  olives, capers, eggplants and capsicums
400 g freekeh, rinsed
3 tablespoons roughly chopped flat-leaf
  parsley leaves
½ cup basil leaves, torn
juice of ½ lemon
sea salt and black pepper

KALE PESTO

½ bunch of kale leaves, washed thoroughly
1 garlic clove, very finely chopped
½ cup sunflower seeds, toasted
185 ml (¾ cup) extra-virgin olive oil
3 tablespoons grated parmesan
sea salt and black pepper

**CHILLI–PARMESAN
SUNFLOWER SEEDS**

¾ cup sunflower seeds
1 tablespoon extra-virgin olive oil
2 tablespoons grated parmesan
½ teaspoon chilli powder or chilli flakes

SUBSTITUTES/OPTIONS

freekeh: spelt, farro, pearl barley
For gluten free, use quinoa in place
  of freekeh

Roughly chop or tear up the marinated vegetables with your hands. The shape and size is up to you.

Add the freekeh to a large saucepan of salted water and bring to the boil. Reduce the heat to a simmer and cook, uncovered, for 40–45 minutes until the grains are tender. Drain.

To make the pesto, blitz the kale, garlic and sunflower seeds together in a food processor, gradually adding the olive oil along with 1 tablespoon of water, until you have a smooth, green sauce. Stir in the parmesan and season to taste with salt and pepper.

For the chilli–parmesan sunflower seeds, preheat the oven to 150°C. In a bowl, combine the sunflower seeds, olive oil, parmesan and chilli powder or flakes (the heat factor is dependent upon the type of chilli powder you use, so exercise your discretion here and vary the amount according to your preference). Mix well to coat the seeds evenly in the flavourings, spread on a baking tray and bake for 10–12 minutes until the cheese is melted and the seeds are golden.

Combine the freekeh, marinated vegetables and herbs and season with salt and pepper. Squeeze over the lemon juice, spoon over big dollops of the kale pesto and fold through gently. To serve, sprinkle over some chilli–parmesan sunflower seeds (you may have extra, so store them in an airtight jar to snack on later).

SO FRENCHIE

Recently, I left a little of my heart in France. I left it at the boulangerie where I picked up my daily bread (and perhaps snuck in a chocolate and banana croissant or two). I left it at the cafe where they serve bowls of creamy café au lait and the flakiest pastries for breakfast. I left it at the bistro where the chèvre chaud salad kept me coming back for more. I left it at the regional Provençal market where we decadently consumed locally grown autumnal produce and artisanal cheeses. I left it in the quiet town of waterways and cobblestone streets where we meandered aimlessly and happily. France is a revolutionary country in more ways than one, and in their food, they are still a nation that truly goes their own, delicious way.

CUMIN-SPICED CAULIFLOWER WITH FRIED LENTILS AND SPINACH YOGHURT

I first cooked this salad in my (temporary) French kitchen in Isle sur la Sorgue, after a market visit left me with a plump cauliflower, a bag of puy lentils and a crazy hankering for salad! Cumin adds a lovely mellow earthiness to the roasted cauli, while crispy fried lentils and a punchy spinach-laced yoghurt bring a touch of celebration to this salad.

GF | SERVES 4~6

2 cauliflower heads (about 1.5 kg),
   cut into florets
1 tablespoon ground cumin
3–5 tablespoons extra-virgin olive oil
300 g puy lentils, rinsed
1 bay leaf
1 garlic clove, very finely chopped
2 teaspoons ground coriander
1 teaspoon paprika
½ cup coriander leaves, chopped
½ cup mint leaves
3 tablespoons roughly chopped toasted
   almonds (optional)
sea salt and black pepper

SPINACH YOGHURT

1 cup baby spinach leaves, washed
   thoroughly and finely chopped
1 tablespoon salted capers, rinsed
   and finely chopped
375 g (1½ cups) Greek yoghurt
½ cup mint leaves, finely sliced
100 ml extra-virgin olive oil
juice of ½ lemon
sea salt and black pepper

Preheat the oven to 200°C.

Place the cauliflower on a large baking tray, sprinkle over the cumin, drizzle over 1–2 tablespoons of olive oil and mix well. Season with salt and pepper and roast for 25–30 minutes until golden.

Meanwhile, bring a large saucepan of water to the boil, add the lentils and bay leaf and cook for 20–25 minutes, until the lentils are just tender. Drain.

To make the spinach yoghurt, whizz together the spinach, capers, yoghurt, mint and olive oil in a food processor. Squeeze over the lemon juice and season well with salt and pepper.

Heat 1 tablespoon of olive oil in a frying pan, add the garlic, ground coriander, paprika and cooked lentils. Season well with sea salt and sauté over a medium–high heat, shaking the pan to move the lentils around and adding another tablespoon of olive oil if needed, until the lentils are slightly crispy.

Spread the spinach yoghurt out onto a large serving platter. Combine the roasted cauliflower with the fried lentils and herbs, drizzle with olive oil and season well with salt and pepper. Spoon the cauliflower mixture over the yoghurt and top with the almonds, if using.

PARSLEY, MACHE AND COMTE PESTO WITH ROASTED BRUSSELS SPROUTS, GREEN BEANS AND QUINOA

This salad celebrates the beautiful autumnal produce found at the local markets in Isle sur la Sorgue, just outside of Avignon, France. During this season, parsley is practically the only herb you see, mache (also known as lamb's lettuce or corn salad) is at its mellow best and comte cheese (my all-time favourite breed of fromage) is in abundant supply. This all makes for a pretty delicious salad!

GF | SERVES 4~6

1 kg brussels sprouts, trimmed and halved
2–3 tablespoons extra-virgin olive oil
200 g white or red quinoa
    (or a mixture), rinsed
375 ml (1½ cups) vegetable stock
250 g green beans, trimmed
½ cup pitted black olives, torn
½ cup flat-leaf parsley leaves,
    roughly chopped
sea salt and black pepper

PARSLEY, MACHE AND COMTE PESTO

1 small garlic clove, roughly chopped
¾ cup flat-leaf parsley leaves,
    roughly chopped
1 cup mache (lamb's lettuce)
40 g almonds (or pine nuts),
    roughly chopped
125 ml (½ cup) extra-virgin olive oil
zest and juice of ½ lemon
40 g comte cheese, grated
sea salt and black pepper

SUBSTITUTES

comte: gruyere, cheddar
mache (lamb's lettuce): baby rocket leaves,
    spinach leaves

Preheat the oven to 200°C.

To make the pesto, place the garlic in a mortar and sprinkle over a good pinch of salt. Pound with the pestle to form a paste, then add the parsley and mache and pound until the leaves have broken down. Add the nuts and pound again to a rough paste, then slowly pour over the oil and stir together until smooth. Add the lemon zest and juice and the cheese and season with salt and pepper to taste.

Place the brussels sprouts on a baking tray, drizzle with 1–2 tablespoons of oil and season with salt and pepper. Roast for 20–25 minutes until tender and golden.

Add the quinoa and vegetable stock to a saucepan and bring to a gentle boil. Reduce the heat to low and leave to simmer for 15 minutes, or until the quinoa is tender and translucent and all the liquid has been absorbed (if there is any liquid left over at this point simply drain it off). Leave the quinoa in the hot saucepan off the heat for 5–10 minutes to allow it to dry out, then fluff up the grains with a fork.

In a frying pan, heat 1 tablespoon of olive oil and add the green beans with a pinch of salt. Sauté for 3–4 minutes, until the beans are just tender and starting to turn golden.

Combine the brussels sprouts, beans, quinoa and olives. Spoon over the pesto and stir well, then scatter over the parsley to finish.

PROVENÇAL EGGPLANT WITH ROASTED CAPSICUM, ZUCCHINI, GREEN BEANS AND PUY LENTILS

Our recent time spent in France has really changed the way I view food. Most importantly, it has highlighted the joys of simple eating – spectacular meals made from humble ingredients. This salad was conceived during our visit to the Provençal neighbourhood of Isle sur la Sorgue. Here, against the backdrop of charming waterways and picturesque autumnal sunsets, our twice-weekly ritual of visiting the local produce markets gave us incredible cooking inspiration. This salad is inspired by Provençal ratatouille and is enjoyed with French lentils, rocket and salty, wilted black olives.

VG | GF | SERVES 4~6

8–9 tablespoons extra-virgin olive oil
2 large eggplants (about 1.1 kg), halved
   lengthways and sliced diagonally into
   1 cm pieces
2 zucchini (about 500 g), sliced diagonally
   into 1 cm pieces
1 onion, finely sliced
1 garlic clove, very finely chopped
2 red capsicums (about 450 g), deseeded
   and sliced into thin strips
4 roma tomatoes (about 500 g),
   roughly chopped
1 tablespoon red wine vinegar
2 teaspoons herbes de Provençe
200 g green beans, trimmed and halved
300 g puy lentils, rinsed
½ cup pitted black olives (preferable
   wrinkly ones), torn in half
2 cups baby rocket leaves
½ cup flat-leaf parsley leaves, finely chopped
sea salt and black pepper

SUBSTITUTES

red capsicums: store-bought chargrilled
   capsicums
herbes de Provençe: dried basil, marjoram,
   rosemary, parsley, oregano or thyme

Preheat the oven to 200°C.

Before roasting, I like to shallow-fry the eggplant and zucchini to soften them and start the process of caramelisation. Heat 1–2 tablespoons of olive oil in a large frying pan. Add some of the eggplant slices in a single layer, sprinkle with a little salt and pan-fry, turning often, until slightly softened and golden on both sides. Repeat, adding more olive oil between batches, until all the eggplant slices have been cooked, then repeat with the zucchini. Set aside.

In a large roasting tin, combine the onion, garlic, capsicum, tomatoes, red wine vinegar, herbes de Provençe and 4 tablespoons of olive oil. Season with salt and pepper and roast for 25 minutes until the tomatoes and capsicum are soft. Remove the tomatoes and capsicum from the tin, add the eggplant, zucchini and green beans and roast for another 20–25 minutes, until all the vegetables are very tender. Season to taste.

Bring a large saucepan of water to the boil, add the lentils and a big pinch of salt and simmer over a medium heat for around 20 minutes or until the lentils are tender but still have a bite to them. Drain.

To serve, combine the roasted vegetables with the lentils, olives, rocket and parsley. Season well and finish with a good drizzle of oil.

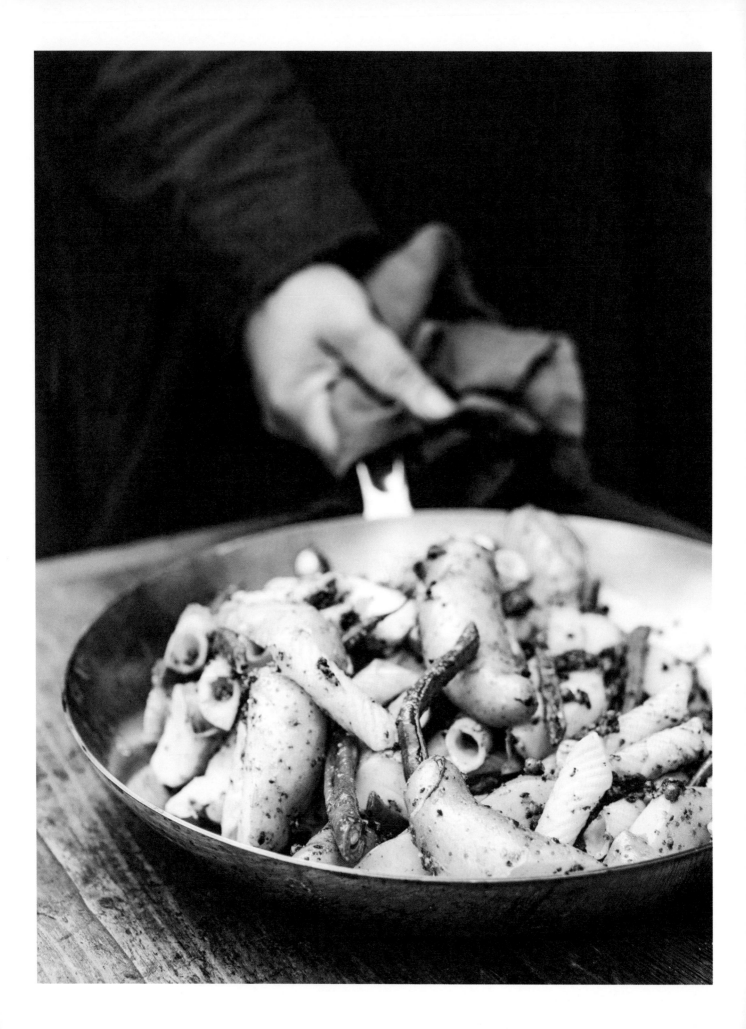

BASIL-OLIVE TAPENADE WITH POTATOES, PASTA, GREEN BEANS AND CAPERS

This salad is perfect picnic or barbecue fare, marrying two outdoor dining staples – potato salad and pasta salad – into one very tasty offering. The delicious basil-scented olive tapenade is wonderful slathered on just cooked, still warm potatoes and pasta. This salad is on the starchy side, but it is extremely satisfying and you may find it popular with all of the family, even the young ones. Experiment with your favourite potato variety and pasta shape.

VG | SERVES 4~6

700 g kipfler potatoes or other medium-
 sized waxy potatoes, halved
500 g short pasta (such as penne,
 orecchiette or rigatoni)
2 tablespoons extra-virgin olive oil
200 g green beans, trimmed and halved
3 tablespoons sunflower seeds, toasted
60 g salted capers, rinsed
½ cup flat-leaf parsley leaves, finely chopped
sea salt

BASIL-OLIVE TAPENADE

2 garlic cloves
1 cup basil leaves
½ cup pitted black olives
 (preferably wrinkly ones)
½ cup walnuts, toasted
80 ml (⅓ cup) extra-virgin olive oil
1 teaspoon white wine vinegar
sea salt and black pepper

SUBSTITUTES

kipfler potatoes: sweet potato,
 Jerusalem artichokes
green beans: asparagus, garden peas

To make the tapenade, place the garlic in a mortar, sprinkle over a pinch of salt and pound with a pestle to form a paste. Add the basil and pound until the leaves have broken down, then add the olives and walnuts and pound again until you get a thick paste. Stir in the olive oil and vinegar and season with pepper. (Alternatively, you can always throw these ingredients in a food processor and blitz away.)

Bring a large saucepan of salted water to the boil, add the potatoes and cook for 15–20 minutes until they are just tender – the exact cooking time will depend on the size and variety of your potatoes so keep an eye on them, as you don't want them so soft that they are breaking apart. When ready, drain.

Bring another saucepan of salted water to the boil. Add the pasta and cook according to the packet instructions until al dente. Drain and combine the warm pasta with the warm potatoes.

Heat 1 tablespoon of olive oil in a frying pan, add the green beans and sauté for 4–5 minutes until the beans are bright green, just tender and beginning to colour.

Combine the tapenade, pasta, potatoes and beans along with a swirl of olive oil to loosen everything up. Toss together well. To serve, scatter over the sunflower seeds, capers and parsley.

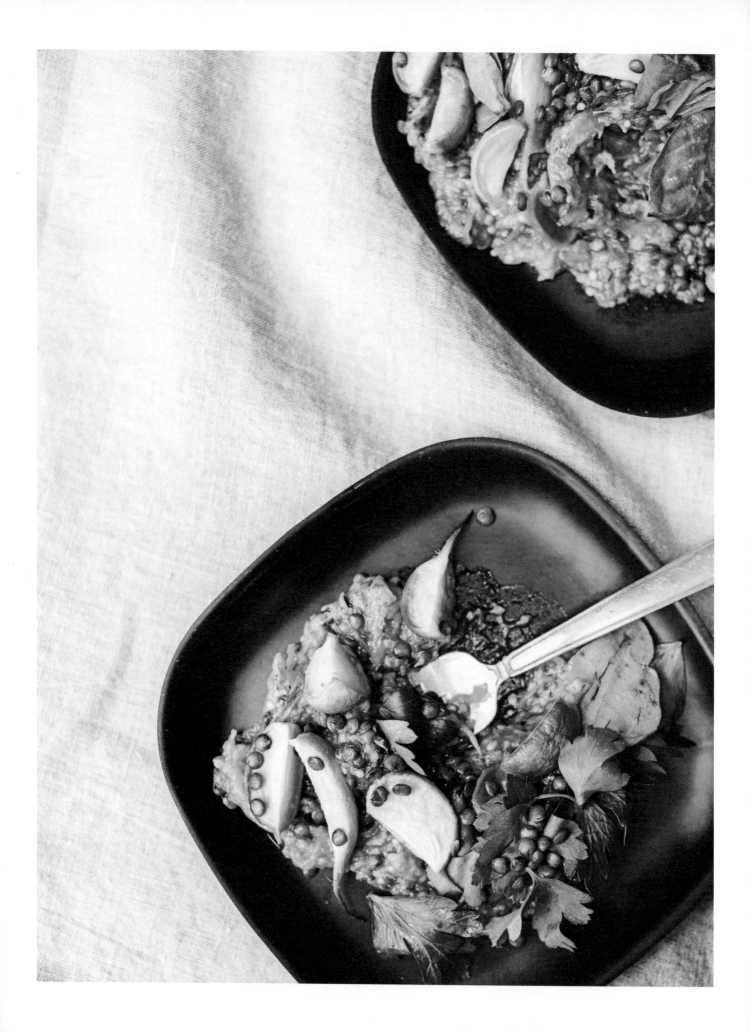

SMASHED EGGPLANT WITH LENTILS AND MAPLE-ROASTED RADISH

While in Provence, I heard about a regally monikered local dish called 'eggplant caviar' that immediately sparked my interest. While it is actually just a simple eggplant dip, this dish encapsulates the respect shown to fresh produce in regional French cuisine. My take on eggplant caviar is lighter than baba ghanoush and is a lovely accompaniment to these rather spectacular roasted radishes. Sneak some of the smashed eggplant aside to use as a dip!

VG | GF | SERVES 4~6

400 g lentils (any variety), rinsed
1 bay leaf
1 small garlic clove, peeled (optional)
30 radishes (about 1 kg), trimmed
    and quartered
1 tablespoon maple syrup
juice of 1 lemon
2 cups baby spinach leaves
½ cup flat-leaf parsley leaves
2 tablespoons extra-virgin olive oil
sea salt and black pepper

SMASHED EGGPLANT

3 eggplants (about 1.2 kg)
125 ml (½ cup) extra-virgin olive oil
1 small garlic clove, grated
juice of 1 lemon, plus extra if necessary
1 eschalot (see note page 32), finely diced
½ teaspoon paprika
½ teaspoon chilli powder
2 tablespoons finely chopped flat-leaf
    parsley leaves
2 tablespoons finely chopped mint leaves
sea salt and black pepper

SUBSTITUTES

maple syrup: honey, agave syrup

To make the smashed eggplant, place the eggplants directly on the flame of a gas hob, over a very hot barbecue, or in an oven preheated to 220°C. Cook, turning often, until they become very soft and the skin is charred all over (this process takes a while, especially when using an open flame, so be patient!). When cool enough to handle, carefully peel the charred skin off the eggplants. Place the eggplant flesh in a large bowl and break it up with a fork. Add the olive oil, garlic, lemon juice, eschalot, paprika, chilli powder and a large pinch of salt and mash everything together, then stir in the parsley and mint. Taste and add more lemon or salt as necessary (the eggplant needs liberal seasoning, so don't be afraid of adding more salt if needed). Alternatively, place everything in the bowl of a food processor and whizz it together.

Bring a large pot of water to the boil, add the lentils, bay leaf, whole garlic clove, if using, and a big pinch of salt and cook for 20–25 minutes until just tender. Drain.

Place the radishes on a large baking tray and drizzle over the maple syrup and half the lemon juice. Toss to combine and roast in the oven for 20–25 minutes until the radishes are tender.

Combine the radishes with the lentils, spinach leaves, parsley, olive oil and the remaining lemon juice and season with salt and pepper. To serve, spread the smashed eggplant over a large serving dish and top with the radishes and lentils.

KINDA-NIÇOISE WITH FRIED GREEN BEANS, ROASTED KALE, LENTILS, STEAMED EGGS AND CAPER MAYO

There is much to love about a classic salade niçoise. As with many rustic French salads, niçoise traditionally brims with the freshest local produce – olives, oil-cured tuna, anchovies and tender green beans. My version celebrates the traditional salty, acidic, green-ness of a classic niçoise, bringing in unbelievably soft, silky steamed eggs as my protein component. Steaming eggs is a nifty little trick I learned from my friend Elham Abi-Ghanem, the best egg cook I know!

GF | SERVES 4~6

6 large eggs, at room temperature
200 g puy lentils, rinsed
2–3 tablespoons extra-virgin olive oil
150 g green beans, trimmed and halved
1 bunch of kale leaves, washed thoroughly,
    central stems removed, leaves torn
½ cup basil leaves, torn
½ cup flat-leaf parsley leaves
1 tablespoon tarragon leaves
½ small red onion, very finely sliced
3 radishes (about 100 g), very finely sliced
200 g cherry tomatoes, halved
½ cup pitted black olives (whichever
    variety), torn
2 teaspoons red wine vinegar
sea salt and black pepper

CAPER MAYONNAISE

250 g (1 cup) whole-egg mayonnaise
125 g (½ cup) natural yoghurt
1 tablespoon extra-virgin olive oil
1 tablespoon salted capers, rinsed and
    roughly chopped
squeeze of lemon juice
1 small garlic clove, very finely chopped
sea salt and black pepper

SUBSTITUTE

puy lentils: another variety of lentil

To make the caper mayonnaise, whisk together the mayonnaise, yoghurt and olive oil until well combined. Stir in the capers, lemon juice and garlic and season with pepper and a little salt to taste (you shouldn't need much salt as the capers will already make this quite salty).

Fill a saucepan with water to a depth of 3 cm and sit a steamer basket on the top. Place the eggs in the steamer basket, cover with a lid and bring the water to the boil. Steam the eggs for around 5 minutes for soft-boiled, 7 minutes for medium or around 9 minutes for hard-boiled. (Of course, the amount of time will depend on the size of your eggs, so you may have to try this a few times to get it perfect for you!) When ready, immediately cool under cold running water.

Add the lentils to a saucepan of salted water, bring to the boil and cook for 20–25 minutes until just tender. Drain.

In a large frying pan, add 1 tablespoon of olive oil and fry the green beans for 3–4 minutes until they are just tender and are starting to char. Remove the beans from the pan and add another tablespoon of oil, then add the kale and cook for a few minutes until wilted and starting to colour.

Combine the beans, kale and herbs with the red onion, radishes, tomatoes, olives and lentils. Pour over the red wine vinegar, drizzle with some olive oil and season with salt and pepper. To serve, pile the salad on a serving dish and drizzle the caper mayo over the top. Peel the eggs, then break up or slice them and place over the salad, finishing with a few good grinds of pepper.

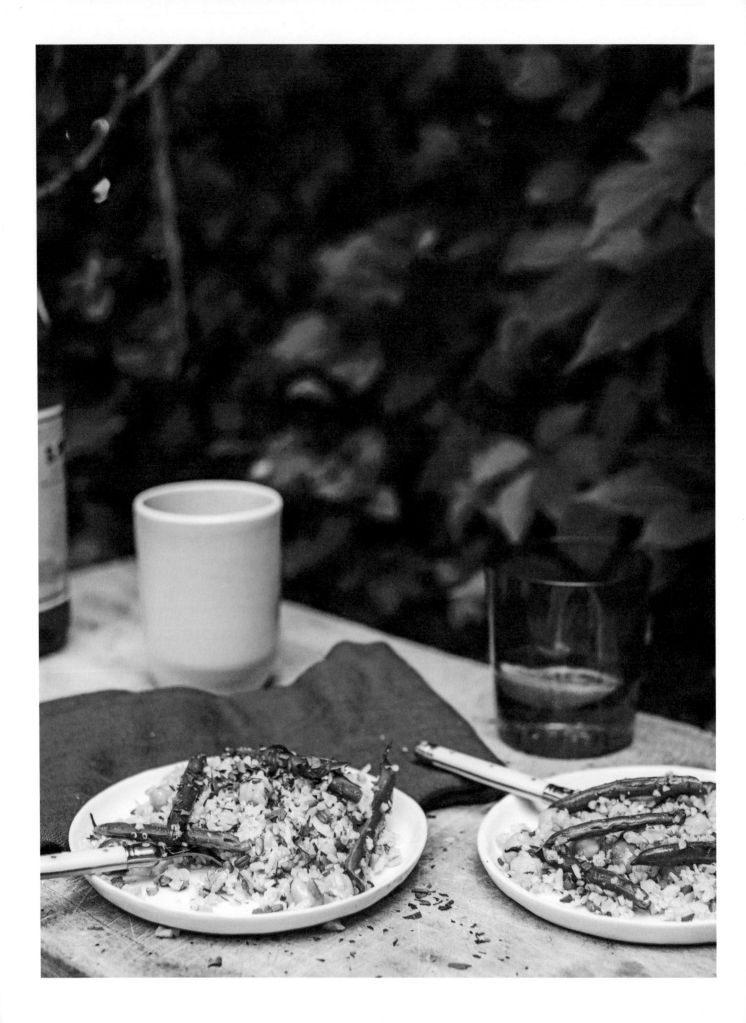

PROVENÇAL GRAIN SALAD WITH GREEN BEANS AND LEMON–PARSLEY OIL

This is a salad I cooked regularly during our stay in Provence, using locally grown red rice from Camargue. This hearty grain salad can be enjoyed warm during the cooler months, but is also lovely served at room temperature for warm summer days. The lemon–parsley oil provides a beautiful citrus lift to the dish. Use other herbs for the oil if you wish – basil, oregano, tarragon or chives also work well.

VG | SERVES 4~6

100 g Camargue red rice
200 g brown rice
100 g quinoa (white, red or a mix), rinsed
100 g coarse bulgur wheat (cracked wheat)
1 tablespoon extra-virgin olive oil
200 g green beans, trimmed and cut into
   2 cm pieces
250 g cooked chickpeas (about 1 can),
   drained and rinsed
12 pitted green olives
3 tablespoons finely sliced Chinese shallots
   (see note page 32)
½ cup flat-leaf parsley leaves, finely chopped
3 tablespoons walnuts, toasted and crushed
sea salt and black pepper

LEMON-PARSLEY OIL

1 small garlic clove, very finely chopped
½ cup flat-leaf parsley leaves, chopped
3 tablespoons extra-virgin olive oil
1 tablespoon walnut oil (or other neutral
   oil like grapeseed)
squeeze of lemon juice
sea salt and black pepper

SUBSTITUTES

Camargue red rice: wild rice, black rice

Add the red and brown rice to a saucepan with 1.5 litres (6 cups) of water and a big pinch of salt. Cover with a lid and bring to the boil over a medium–high heat, then reduce the heat to a simmer and leave to cook for 15–20 minutes, until the grains are soft and all the water has been absorbed (if there is any water left at this point, simply drain it away). If you prefer, you can cook this in a rice cooker instead.

Combine the quinoa and bulgur wheat and cook them in 500 ml (2 cups) of salted water until soft, draining off any remaining water as before. Leave the mixture to sit in the hot saucepan for 5–10 minutes to dry out and fluff up.

Heat the olive oil in a small frying pan over a high heat, add the beans and fry with a pinch of salt for 4–5 minutes until tender and starting to brown. Leave to cool.

To make the lemon–parsley oil, add the garlic and 1 teaspoon of salt to a mortar and pound together with a paste to form a rough paste. Add the parsley and pound until the leaves are broken down and the paste is green, then stir in the oils and lemon juice and season to taste with salt and pepper.

Combine the red rice, brown rice, quinoa, bulgur wheat, chickpeas, green beans, green olives, shallot and parsley in a big bowl and stir well, then season with salt and pepper. To serve, scatter over the walnuts and drizzle over the lemon–parsley oil.

ROASTED CHESTNUTS WITH PAN-FRIED PEARS, BLUE CHEESE, WITLOF AND MUSTARD VINAIGRETTE

Provincial markets are the lifeblood of big and small towns all over France, and are vital in providing locals with their daily necessities. There are no fancy food providores here, this is real food – grown, made and baked locally. In the autumn, markets in Provence are abundant with chestnuts, pears and witlof, so this is my version of a French market salad. The chestnuts take a little time to prepare, but while they are roasting they will fill your house with the sweetest aroma that makes it totally worth the effort.

GF | SERVES 4~6

500 g chestnuts
20 g salted butter
1 tablespoon honey
3 thyme sprigs
5 beurre bosc pears (about 1.1 kg),
   cores removed, peeled and each
   cut into 8 wedges
1 butter lettuce, leaves picked apart
2 witlof, leaves picked apart and torn
3 tablespoons finely chopped chives
3 tablespoons finely chopped flat-leaf
   parsley leaves
200 g soft blue cheese, crumbled
¼ cup hazelnuts, toasted, skinned
   and roughly chopped
sea salt and black pepper

MUSTARD VINAIGRETTE

1 tablespoon dijon mustard
2 tablespoons cider vinegar
2 tablespoons honey
80 ml (⅓ cup) extra-virgin olive oil
1 garlic clove, very finely chopped
sea salt and black pepper

Preheat the oven to 180°C.

Prepare the chestnuts by scoring them with a sharp knife, working your way around their circumference and being careful not to cut too deep into the flesh. (Scoring the chestnuts like this helps the skin to come off once they are cooked.)

Place the scored chestnuts on a large baking tray and roast in the oven for 25–30 minutes, until the tough outer skins have cracked open and the insides are tender. While they are still hot, peel away the outer skins and the papery skins inside.

Melt the butter together with the honey and thyme sprigs in a large frying pan. Add the pears and cook gently for 5 minutes, turning, until softened and starting to brown.

To make the mustard vinaigrette, whisk together all the ingredients and season with salt and pepper.

Combine the butter lettuce and witlof leaves with the chestnuts, chives and parsley. Add the vinaigrette, season lightly with salt and pepper and toss together. Arrange the salad on a large serving platter and top with the pears and the cooking syrup from the pan. Dot with the crumbled blue cheese and scatter over the chopped hazelnuts to finish.

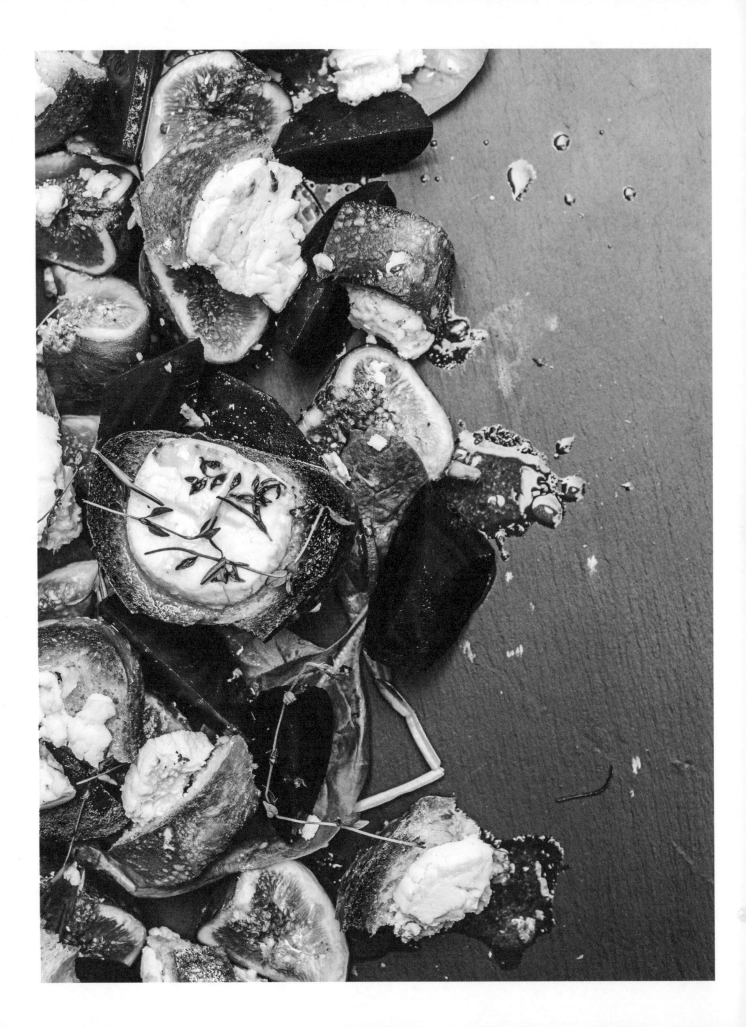

WARM GOAT'S CHEESE CROUTONS WITH ROASTED BEETROOT, FIGS AND APPLE–MUSTARD DRESSING

A trip to Paris invariably means high salade au chèvre chaud *consumption, which is fine by me! In a city where vegetarian food can still be hard to come by, this hot goat's cheese salad has saved me too many times to recall. This is such a beautifully simple salad with the most harmonious flavours. My version includes roasted beetroot, figs and a divine apple–mustard dressing. Use whatever salad leaves you have on hand for this.*

SERVES 4~6

6 small beetroot (about 800 g), peeled and
   cut into small wedges
2 tablespoons extra-virgin olive oil
150 g baguette, sliced into 2 cm thick rounds
200 g goat's cheese log, rind on
5 thyme sprigs, leaves picked
2 teaspoons chopped rosemary leaves
3 cups watercress
3 cups mache (lamb's lettuce)
3 tablespoons chopped chives
4 figs, each cut into 8 segments
1 cup walnuts, toasted and crushed
sea salt and black pepper

APPLE–MUSTARD DRESSING

3 tablespoons apple juice
2 tablespoons extra-virgin olive oil
1 tablespoon honey
1 tablespoon dijon mustard
1 tablespoon cider vinegar
1 small garlic clove, very finely chopped
sea salt and black pepper

SUBSTITUTES

mache (lamb's lettuce): baby spinach leaves
watercress: baby rocket leaves

Preheat the oven to 200°C.

Spread the beetroot on a large baking tray, drizzle with 1 tablespoon of olive oil, season with salt and pepper and roast for 30–35 minutes until tender.

Preheat the grill to high. Place the baguette slices on a baking tray, drizzle over 1 tablespoon of olive oil and place under the hot grill for 2 minutes, or until golden. Remove the croutons from the grill.

Slice the goat's cheese into as many rounds as you have croutons. Place a slice of cheese on the un-grilled side of each crouton and top with a few thyme and rosemary leaves. Return to the grill and cook for 3–4 minutes, or until the goat's cheese is soft and golden.

To make the dressing, whisk together all the ingredients and season with salt and pepper to taste.

Toss the salad leaves together with the chives. To serve, arrange the beetroot slices and figs on top of the leaves, drizzle over the apple–mustard dressing and season with salt and pepper. Top with the goat's cheese croutons and the walnuts.

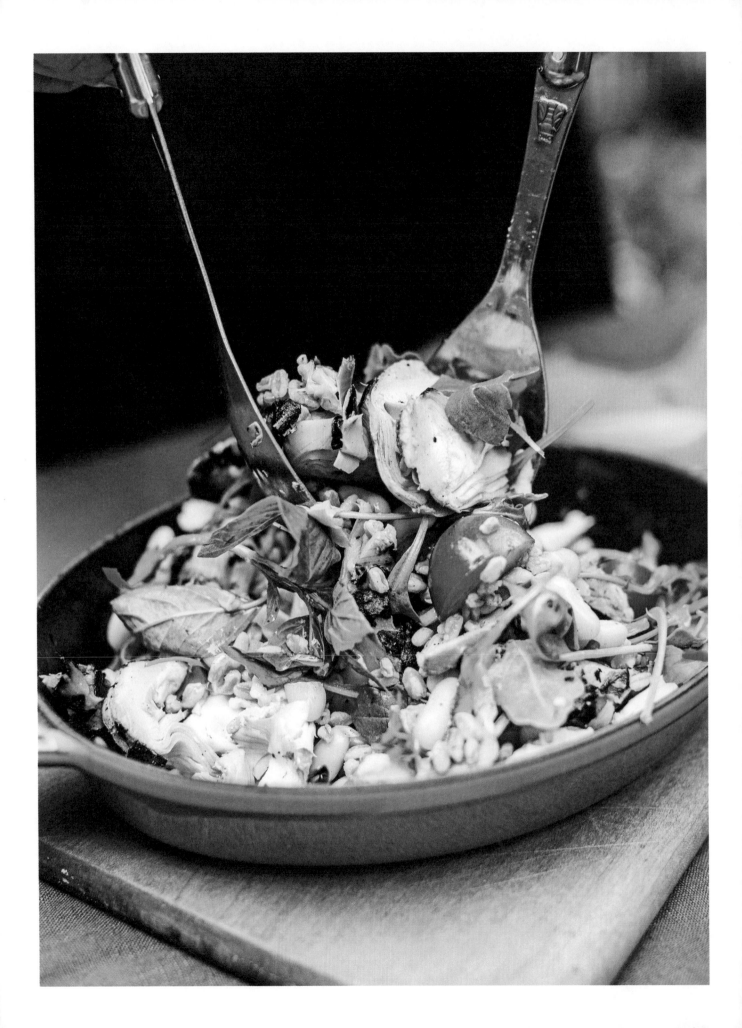

GLOBE ARTICHOKES WITH CANNELLINI BEANS, CHERRY TOMATOES, LEMON AND BUFFALO MOZZARELLA

For years, I resisted the urge to cook globe artichokes. Their natural thistled beauty fascinated me, but, to be honest, I wondered if all that preparation was really worth it. But while in Provence, with time and patience on our side and armed with beautiful globes from the local market, our family finally discovered the joys of freshly prepared artichokes. And yes, they are most definitely worth the effort. Try this once and you'll be hooked (though if you can't be bothered, store-bought marinated artichokes hearts are fine too!).

SERVES 4~6

zest and juice of 1 lemon
6 globe artichokes (about 1.3 kg)
400 g spelt grains
2–3 tablespoons extra-virgin olive oil
1 garlic clove, very finely chopped
1 tablespoon finely chopped rosemary leaves
2 teaspoons finely chopped oregano leaves
250 g cherry tomatoes, halved
500 g cooked cannellini beans (about
    2 cans), drained
2 cups baby rocket leaves
300 g buffalo mozzarella, torn into chunks
1 long red chilli, deseeded and sliced into
    very thin strips
½ cup basil leaves, torn
3 tablespoons pine nuts, toasted
sea salt and black pepper

Begin by preparing the artichokes. Squeeze half the lemon juice into a large bowl of water. Trim the artichoke stalks to about 3 cm in length, then slice about 2 cm off the top of each globe. Peel away and discard the outer two or three layers of the artichoke until you get to the inner yellow leaves, then trim around the stalk with a paring knife, peeling away the tough outer skin. Cut the artichokes in half, carefully remove and discard the furry chokes and place the artichoke halves in the bowl of lemon water to stop them browning.

Bring a pot of salted water to the boil. Add the spelt grains and cook for 20–25 minutes until tender. Drain.

Slice the prepared artichoke halves into thin wedges. Heat 1–2 tablespoons of olive oil in a large frying pan over a medium–high heat, add the garlic, rosemary and oregano leaves and cook until fragrant, about 30 seconds. Add the artichoke pieces along with a big pinch of salt and pepper and sauté for 4–5 minutes, adding a splash of water halfway through cooking, until tender.

Combine the tomatoes, cannellini beans, spelt grains and rocket leaves and spread the mixture evenly over a large serving plate or platter. Dot the artichokes, mozzarella, chilli strips and torn basil over the salad, then add the lemon zest and the remaining lemon juice. To serve, season well with sea salt and black pepper, drizzle with olive oil and scatter over the pine nuts.

INTO THE MEDITERRANEAN

Into the Mediterranean we go, alive with blue skies, pebble shores, cerulean seas, bucolic settings and sun-blistered skin. Memories of vacations amongst the flaxen hillsides and soaring mountains of bountiful Italy and Spain, rapaciously feeding upon the Mediterranean diet of plump tomatoes, creamy cheeses, fresh pasta, bright herbs, perky citrus and sharp acids. Salty olives and capers enliven nourishing grains and legumes. Crusty bread a must at every meal. Each and every dish completed by lashings of earthy olive oil. The Mediterranean way to eat is perfectly simple and simply perfect.

CHARGRILLED BROCCOLI, ZUCCHINI, PEAS AND RADISH WITH CANNELLINI BEANS AND CAPER BAGNA CAUDA

This salad is as green as they come, brimming with the vitality and colour of summer's most abundant vegetables. It features my take on Italian bagna cauda, a traditional Piedmontese dip using capers in place of anchovies. I like my bagna cauda very lemony but vary the amount of juice according to your desires. Serve with some crusty Italian bread to mop up the salty, lemony goodness.

SERVES 4~6

2 small broccoli heads (about 800 g), cut into florets
3 zucchini, sliced diagonally into 5 mm pieces
2–3 tablespoons extra-virgin olive oil
150 g garden peas (fresh or frozen)
500 g cooked cannellini beans (about 2 cans), drained
2 radishes, shaved
½ cup basil leaves, torn
½ cup mint leaves, torn
½ cup flat-leaf parsley leaves, chopped
1 crusty Italian bread loaf, to serve (optional)
sea salt and black pepper

CAPER BAGNA CAUDA

3 garlic cloves
80 g (⅓ cup) salted capers, rinsed
125 ml (½ cup) extra-virgin olive oil
100 g salted butter
zest and juice of 1 lemon

OPTION

For vegans, use olive oil in place of butter

Start by making the caper bagna cauda. Place the garlic cloves and capers in a large mortar and pound with a pestle until you have a chunky paste. Add the caper–garlic paste to a small frying pan along with the olive oil and butter, bring it to a simmer and gently cook for a further 3–4 minutes. Remove from the heat and add the lemon zest and juice, adjusting the amount of citrus according to your personal preference. Keep warm.

Heat a griddle pan or barbecue to high. Coat the broccoli and zucchini in the olive oil and season with a big pinch of salt. Add the broccoli and zucchini to the pan or barbecue and cook, turning occasionally, until tender and slightly charred on all sides.

Bring a small pot of salted water to the boil, add the peas and blanch until just tender, about 1–2 minutes. Drain and refresh under cold running water.

Combine the broccoli, zucchini, peas, cannellini beans and shaved radishes in a large bowl. Add the herbs, a big sprinkle of salt and pepper and toss everything together well. Spoon the warm caper bagna cauda over the top and serve with crusty Italian bread, if you like.

CAPONATA WITH PEARL COUSCOUS AND ALMONDS

During our London years, my husband and I were devout Italophiles, visiting Italy often. One of our favourite places was Sicily. Here, we ate well and cheaply at tucked-away restaurants in Palermo and in the small fishing village called Sciacca, where we would feast on wonderful things like caponata. My take on this Sicilian classic is given a kick with the addition of harissa and is intensely sweet and sour. Feel free to adjust the amount of vinegar and sugar to your liking and taste.

VG | SERVES 4~6

3 small eggplants (about 800 g)
3–4 tablespoons extra-virgin olive oil
3–4 tablespoons sunflower oil
2 red capsicums, deseeded and cut into
    2 cm pieces
3 celery stalks, trimmed and finely sliced
2 onions, finely sliced
1 tablespoon harissa paste (store-bought
    or see my recipe on page 121)
400 g diced tomatoes (about 1 can)
2–3 tablespoons red wine vinegar
2 tablespoons salted capers, rinsed
½ cup pitted green Sicilian olives
2–3 teaspoons caster sugar
juice of ½ lemon
500 g pearl couscous
½ cup flat-leaf parsley leaves, finely chopped
½ cup slivered almonds, toasted
sea salt and black pepper

OPTION

For gluten free, use quinoa or brown rice
    in place of couscous

Peel strips of skin from the eggplants, from top to bottom, so it leaves a stripy pattern. Cut the eggplants into 2 cm cubes.

Heat 2 tablespoons each of the olive and sunflower oils in a large casserole dish. Add the eggplant and fry for 3–4 minutes over a medium heat, turning often, until golden (you may have to do this in several batches to avoid overcrowding). Remove the eggplant from the dish and place in a colander. Sprinkle over some salt.

Add the capsicum and celery to the casserole dish along with an extra tablespoon of sunflower oil if needed, and fry for 3 minutes until slightly softened. Season with a pinch of salt, then transfer to the colander with the eggplant.

Heat 1 tablespoon of olive oil in the casserole dish and add the onions. Cook for 2 minutes, then stir in the harissa paste and cook for another 5 minutes, or until the onions are soft. Return the eggplant, celery and capsicum to the pan and add the tomatoes, red wine vinegar, capers and olives. Stir in the sugar and season with salt and pepper. If the mixture is a bit dry, add a few tablespoons of water (though just a little at a time, as the mixture will become more liquid as the vegetables cook). Cover and cook for 20 minutes over a low–medium heat, or until the vegetables are soft. When cooked, squeeze in some lemon juice and taste, seasoning again with salt and pepper if required.

Bring a large pot of salted water to the boil. Add the pearl couscous and cook for 8–10 minutes or until the couscous is tender. Drain.

In a large mixing bowl, spoon the caponata over the couscous and fold together so that the vegetables and sauce coat the balls of couscous. Finish with a drizzle of olive oil and sprinkle over the parsley and almonds.

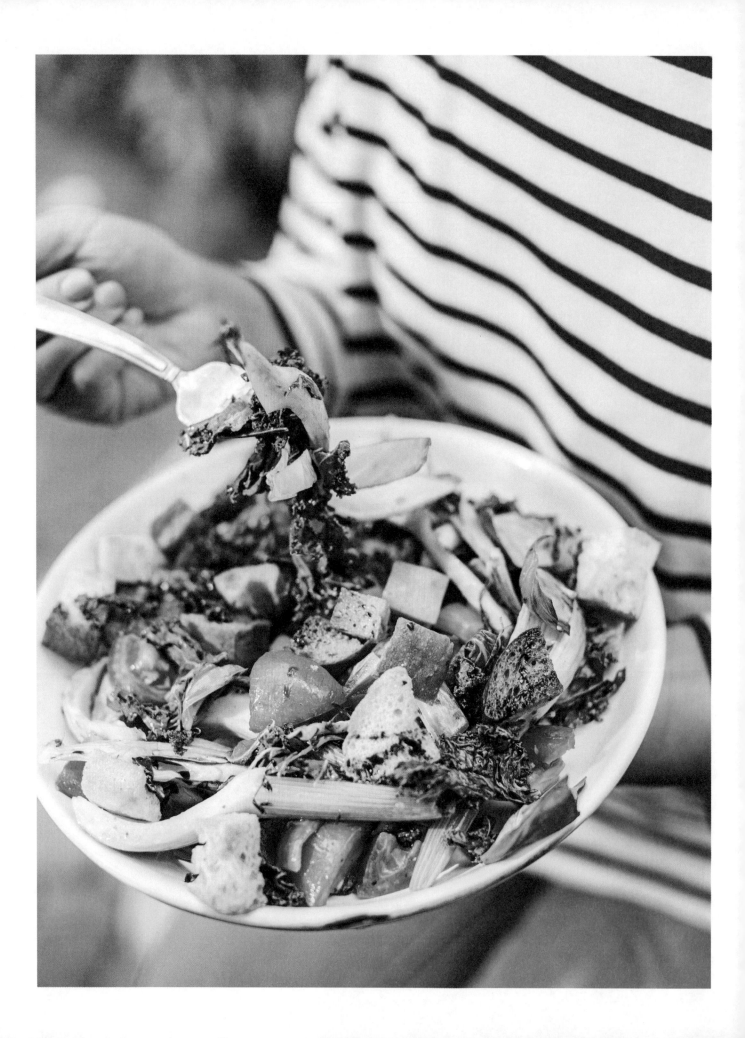

WINTER PANZANELLA WITH ROASTED TOMATOES, FENNEL, KALE AND CARAMELISED BALSAMIC

Apart from being incredibly delicious, I love the practicality of a bread salad. It is the perfect way to use up all those leftover ends of bread loaves. The stars of a classic panzanella are the ripe, juicy tomatoes and the bread. The bread you choose is important – it needs to have a hearty texture with a crunchy crust, so I favour sourdough for this salad. This is a darker, deeper version of panzanella, heavier with vegetables and finished with a super simple-to-make caramelised balsamic vinegar. If you don't have fennel and kale on hand, you could also use other vegetables such as cucumber, zucchini or radish.

VG | SERVES 4~6

400 g stale sourdough bread, torn
  into chunks
100 ml extra-virgin olive oil
5 roma tomatoes (or any variety)
½ red onion, very finely sliced
4 thyme sprigs, leaves picked
½ teaspoon caster sugar
3 fennel bulbs (about 1.2 kg), cut into
  thick wedges
1 garlic clove, very finely chopped
½ bunch of kale leaves, washed thoroughly,
  central stems removed, leaves torn
3 tablespoons roughly chopped flat-leaf
  parsley leaves
½ cup basil leaves, torn
1 tablespoon oregano leaves
80 ml (⅓ cup) Caramelised Balsamic
  Vinegar (see below)
sea salt and black pepper

**CARAMELISED BALSAMIC VINEGAR
(MAKES 175 ML)**

250 ml (1 cup) balsamic vinegar
2 tablespoons soft brown sugar
3 tablespoons caster sugar, plus extra
  if necessary

Preheat the oven to 200°C.

To make the caramelised balsamic, add the vinegar and sugars to a small saucepan and heat gently until the sugars have dissolved. Increase the heat to high, bring to the boil and cook for 5–10 minutes until the mixture has thickened and reduced by about half. Test it by placing a small amount on a cold spoon – it should look darker and run on the spoon less easily. This is a good opportunity to test it for sweetness, adding more caster sugar if you desire. It will thicken further upon cooling.

Place the bread chunks on a large baking tray, drizzle over 2 tablespoons of olive oil and sprinkle over a pinch of salt. Bake for 15 minutes, tossing halfway through, until the bread is golden and crispy on all sides.

Cut the tomatoes into chunks about 2 cm in size. Place them in a bowl with the red onion, thyme leaves, 1 tablespoon of olive oil and the sugar. Mix everything together well and season with salt and pepper. Set aside.

Spread the fennel over a large baking tray. Drizzle over 1 tablespoon of olive oil, season with salt and pepper and roast for 20 minutes or until starting to turn golden. Spread the tomato and red onion mixture over the fennel pieces and roast for another 10–15 minutes until the tomatoes are softened and almost ready to collapse.

Heat 1 tablespoon of olive oil in a frying pan, add the garlic, kale and a small pinch of salt and cook for 4–5 minutes until the kale leaves are wilted and starting to turn golden and crispy.

Combine the roasted vegetables with the croutons, kale and herbs and season with salt and pepper. Drizzle over the caramelised balsamic and toss together. Let the salad sit for 20–30 minutes or so to allow the flavours to soak into the bread, or eat straight away if you can't resist!

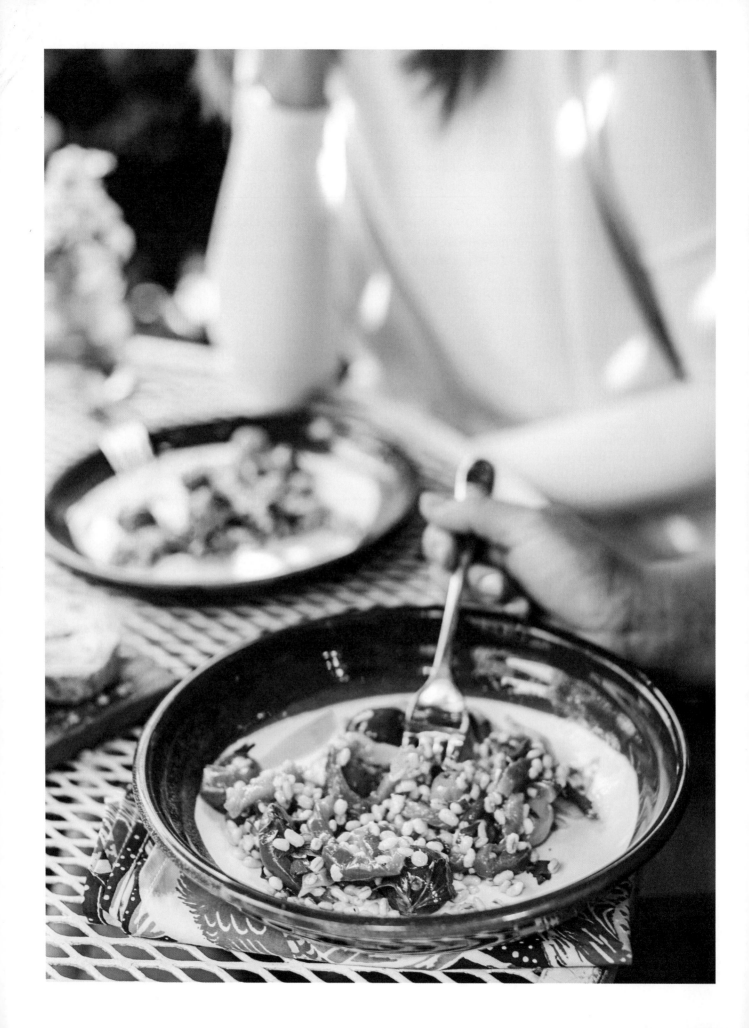

ROASTED CAPSICUM AND CHERRY TOMATOES WITH PEARL BARLEY, CUMIN AND SHERRY VINEGAR

Roasting dramatically intensifies the character of capsicums, bringing out their natural sweetness and piquancy. Here, the natural roasting juices of the capsicums, tomatoes and onions cleverly morph into the salad dressing. This dish was inspired by one of my dearest friends, Davida Sweeney, who often extolls the delights of roasted capsicums drenched in olive oil and sherry vinegar, as is served in her native Spain.

SERVES 4~6

12 red capsicums (about 2.4 kg), halved
    and deseeded
2 onions, each cut into 8 wedges
4 garlic cloves, unpeeled
4–5 tablespoons extra-virgin olive oil
400 g cherry tomatoes, halved
400 g pearl barley, rinsed
3 tablespoons roughly chopped flat-leaf
    parsley leaves
1 teaspoon caster sugar
2 tablespoons sherry vinegar
1 teaspoon ground cumin
½ cup almonds, toasted and
    roughly chopped
80 g manchego cheese, shaved
sea salt and black pepper

SUBSTITUTES

red capsicums: yellow or orange capsicums
manchego cheese: parmesan or pecorino

Preheat the oven to 200°C.

Arrange the capsicum halves, cut-side down, in two large roasting tins along with the onion wedges and garlic cloves. Drizzle over 2–3 tablespoons of olive oil and season with salt and pepper. Roast for 35–40 minutes, adding the cherry tomatoes to the roasting tins 20 minutes into cooking, until the capsicums are well softened. Remove from the oven and leave to cool.

When cool enough to handle, carefully peel the skin off the capsicums and slice them into strips. Return to the tins with the roasted tomatoes and onions, squeezing the soft garlic flesh out of the skins and mashing it gently into the cooking juices with the back of a fork. Stir to combine.

Add the pearl barley and a big pinch of salt to a large saucepan. Bring to the boil and cook for 25–30 minutes until the barley is swollen and tender. Drain.

While the barley is still warm, add it to the pan with the capsicum, tomatoes and onions and stir to coat the barley in the 'dressing'. Add the parsley, sugar, sherry vinegar and cumin and drizzle with the remaining olive oil. Season with salt and pepper and gently mix together. To serve, sprinkle over the almonds and shaved manchego cheese.

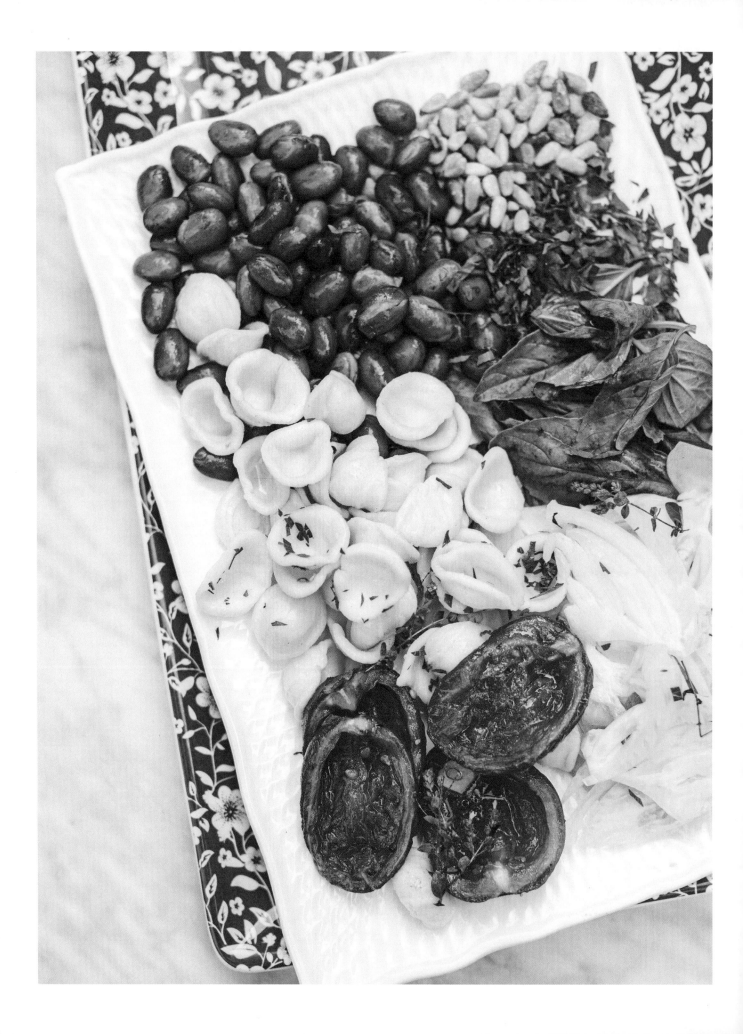

PASTA E FAGIOLI WITH FENNEL
AND CONFIT TOMATOES

One of my favourite things to do in the kitchen is to take a simple, classic concept and turn it into something a little bit special. This salad is a pretty fine example of turning rustic into remarkable, with pantry staples of pasta and beans given a sophisticated lift with dazzling confit tomatoes and crisp shaved fennel. The tomato cooking oil cleverly becomes a rather smashing scented oil to dress the salad. The confit tomatoes can be made a day ahead and stored in the refrigerator – just bring them to room temperature before adding to the salad.

VG | SERVES 4~6

250 g short pasta (such as orecchiette,
   rigatoni, penne or cavatelli)
2 fennel bulbs (about 800 g), finely shaved
500 g cooked borlotti beans
   (about 2 cans), drained
½ cup basil leaves, torn
3 tablespoons finely chopped flat-leaf
   parsley leaves
3 tablespoons roughly chopped
   oregano leaves
3 tablespoons pine nuts, toasted
sea salt and black pepper

CONFIT TOMATOES

8 roma tomatoes (about 1 kg), quartered
   with seeds and membranes removed
5 thyme sprigs
1 bay leaf
3 garlic cloves, unpeeled
1 teaspoon sea salt
125 ml (½ cup) extra-virgin olive oil

Preheat the oven to 150°C.

For the confit tomatoes, choose a baking dish that will fit the tomatoes snugly. Arrange the tomatoes in the dish, scatter over the thyme sprigs, bay leaf and garlic, sprinkle over the salt and pour over the olive oil. Roast for 1 hour 40 minutes, turning the tomatoes over 40 minutes into cooking, until the tomatoes are slightly shrunken but still plump. (The trick is to keep the temperature very low.) Leave the tomatoes to cool completely, reserving the cooking oil, then carefully peel off the skins.

Cook the pasta in a saucepan of boiling salted water, according to packet instructions, until al dente. Drain and refresh under cold, running water.

To serve, combine the pasta, fennel, borlotti beans and herbs and season with salt and pepper. Spoon over the confit tomatoes, pour over the confit cooking oil to flavour the salad and top with the pine nuts.

SLOW-COOKED CHICKPEAS WITH ROASTED CARROTS, SPINACH AND ZA'ATAR

There is a certain quiet elegance to this Mediterranean-inspired dish of slow-cooked chickpeas, patiently roasted in a flavoursome capsicum and tomato puree and colourful spices. The joy in this dish is taking a simple pantry item – canned chickpeas – and turning it into something utterly spectacular.

VG | GF | SERVES 4~6

500 g (2 cups) tomato passata
1 teaspoon caster sugar
750 g cooked chickpeas
   (about 3 cans), drained
10 small carrots (about 800 g), peeled
1–2 tablespoons extra-virgin olive oil
3 cups baby spinach leaves,
   washed thoroughly
½ cup flat-leaf parsley leaves,
   roughly chopped
½ cup mint leaves
1 tablespoon za'atar
sea salt and black pepper

RED PEPPER PASTE

80 ml (⅓ cup) extra-virgin olive oil
1 red onion, roughly chopped
2 garlic cloves, crushed
1 tablespoon tomato paste
1 teaspoon cayenne pepper
½ teaspoon smoked paprika
2 red capsicums, deseeded and
   roughly diced
1 teaspoon sea salt

Preheat the oven to 200°C.

To make the red pepper paste, put all the ingredients in a food processor and blitz.

In a large pan, add the red pepper paste and fry over a medium heat, stirring occasionally, for 5 minutes. Add the tomato passata, sugar, chickpeas and 250 ml (1 cup) of water, bring to a very gentle simmer, cover and cook over a very low heat for 1 hour, stirring from time to time and adding water as needed to maintain a sauce-like consistency (the sauce needs to thicken without the chickpeas becoming dry). When ready, leave to cool.

Place the carrots on a large baking tray, drizzle with the olive oil and season well with salt and pepper. Roast for about 40 minutes until the carrots are tender and starting to turn golden.

To serve, spoon the chickpeas onto a large serving dish, scatter over the baby spinach and arrange the carrots on top. To finish, sprinkle over the herbs and za'atar.

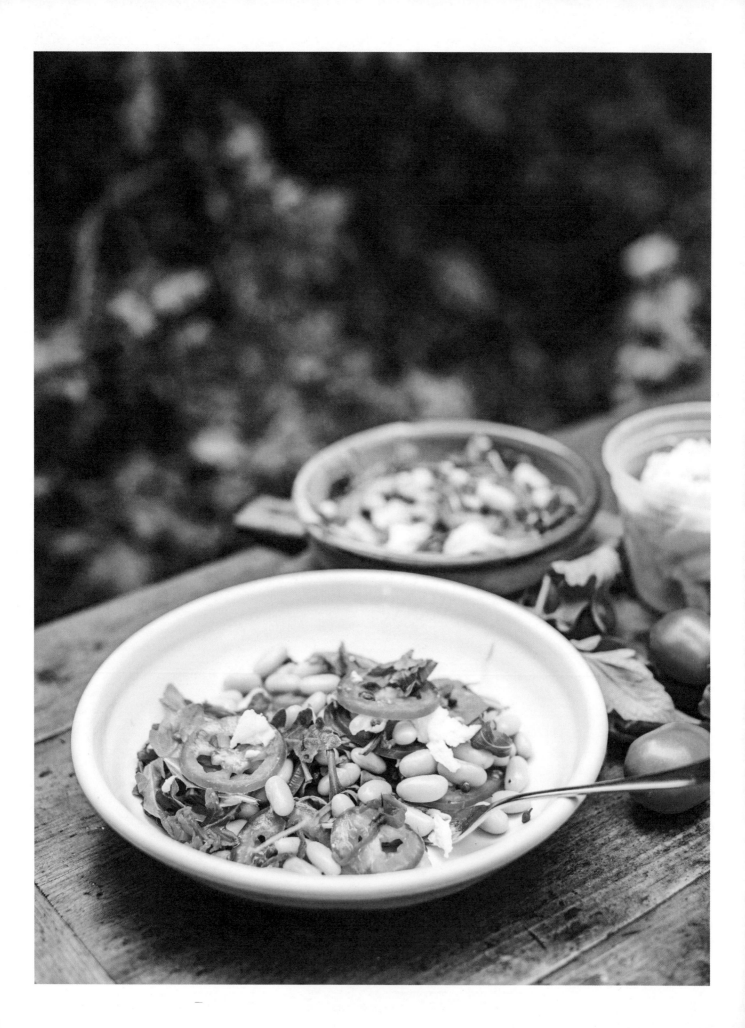

BLACKENED CHILLI WITH BUFFALO MOZZARELLA, CANNELLINI BEANS AND LEMON CRÈME FRAÎCHE

With this salad, I wanted to show the true flavour characteristics of chilli, without diffusing the heat. When charred, chilli exudes a sweet tang, reminiscent of roasted capsicums. The creamy buffalo mozzarella and smooth lemony crème fraîche harmoniously counterbalance the chilli's feistiness, but you can use any fresh white cheese such as bocconcini, fior di latte, burrata or even chunks of ricotta. Make sure you consume this salad (as almost always with salads) at room temperature!

GF | SERVES 4~6

5 long red chillies
2 cups baby rocket leaves
500 g buffalo mozzarella
4 roma tomatoes (about 500 g),
    finely sliced into rounds
500 g cooked cannellini beans
    (about 2 cans), drained
½ cup basil leaves, roughly torn
½ cup salted capers, rinsed
1–2 tablespoons extra-virgin olive oil
juice of ½ lemon
sea salt and black pepper

LEMON CRÈME FRAÎCHE

100 g crème fraîche
zest and juice of ½ lemon, plus extra
    juice if necessary
1 tablespoon extra-virgin olive oil
sea salt and black pepper

SUBSTITUTES

chillies: red or yellow capsicums
buffalo mozzarella: bocconcini,
    fior di latte, burrata, ricotta

Start by blackening the chillies. I do this directly on the naked flame of a gas hob, but you can also place it under a hot grill or on a barbecue. Whichever cooking method you choose, you need to char the skin of the chilli until it's all black and the flesh has softened. Turn the chillies often as the skin will blacken quite quickly. Leave to cool.

When cool enough to handle, wearing gloves, gently rub the blackened skin off the chillies under running water and dry with a paper towel. Cut each chilli in half and carefully scrape away and discard the seeds and membrane. Cut the chilli flesh into thin strips.

To make the lemon crème fraîche, stir the crème fraîche, lemon zest and juice and the olive oil together. Season to taste with salt and pepper and adjust the lemon juice according to your preference.

Scatter the rocket leaves over a large serving plate. Slice or tear the buffalo mozzarella and arrange on top of the rocket. Tuck the sliced tomatoes around the mozzarella and scatter over the cannellini beans, basil leaves, capers and chilli strips. Dollop the lemon crème fraîche over the top, drizzle over a little olive oil, squeeze over some lemon juice and sprinkle with a good pinch of salt and pepper to finish.

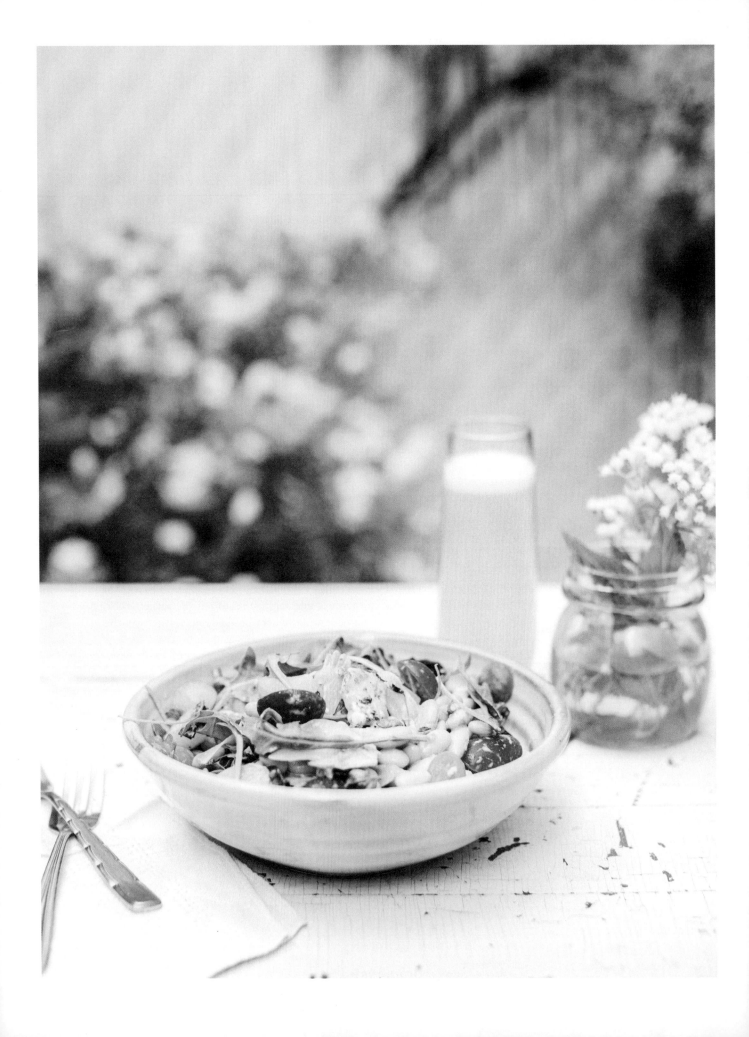

GORGONZOLA-BAKED FENNEL WITH CANNELLINI BEANS, TOMATOES, OLIVES AND PINE NUTS

Blue cheese is one of the most polarising foods. Some love it, many hate it. I have come full circle with my affection for blue cheese. Starting off as a hater, I now adore mouldy blues for their unabashed full-flavoured gutsiness. Gorgonzola, a veined Italian blue cheese, is one of my favourites – creamy, salty and buttery, it is such a lovely accompaniment to vegetables. Here, gorgonzola is baked with fennel, in a surprising Milanese-inspired salad that just might turn you from blue cheese doubter to believer …

GF | SERVES 4~6

2 large fennel bulbs (800 g),
    trimmed and finely sliced
125 ml (½ cup) cream
125 ml (½ cup) vegetable stock
200 g gorgonzola, crumbled
5 thyme sprigs, leaves picked
250 g cherry tomatoes, halved
500 g cooked cannellini beans
    (about 2 cans), drained
½ cup pitted wrinkly black olives, torn
2 cups baby rocket leaves
3 tablespoons roughly chopped flat-leaf
    parsley leaves
¼ cup basil leaves, torn
3 tablespoons pine nuts, toasted
sea salt and black pepper

SUBSTITUTE

gorgonzola: other blue cheese variety

Preheat the oven to 200°C.

Arrange the fennel slices on a large baking tray. Stir the cream and stock together, then pour the mixture over the fennel. Scatter over the gorgonzola and thyme leaves and season with a little salt and pepper. Bake for about 20 minutes until the fennel is just tender and starting to brown. Place the cherry tomatoes on top of the fennel and bake for a further 5 minutes until the tomatoes have softened.

Combine the fennel and tomatoes with the cannellini beans, olives, rocket and herbs. To serve, scatter over the pine nuts.

EAST, MEET WEST

Where East meets West, salad magic is made. This is a melting pot, where influences of the West mingle with flavours from the East, creating dishes of colour and flair. Geographically, Istanbul is where East meets West, a crossroads of civilisations and food. From there, we venture further afield to taste the fresh aromas of olive oil, garlic and lemons in Lebanese cuisine and the passionate herbs and fierce spices of the Middle East. Tomatoes, cucumber, cauliflower and eggplant synthesise gracefully with lashings of thick Greek yoghurt and nutty tahini to produce powerfully flavoured salads. In food, East and West exist in harmony and unity.

ROASTED CAULIFLOWER WITH FARRO, PINE NUTS, MINT AND AGRODOLCE

I learn so much about culture and history through cooking. Agrodolce is said to have been brought to Sicily by the Arabs around the thirteenth century, a time of great cultural appreciation of Sheikh and Emirate traditions. Such experimentation at the time led to the discovery of 'agro' (sour) and 'dolce' (sweet) flavours that have remained strong to this day in Sicily. When I first cooked this salad for Arthur Street Kitchen, it was an instant hit. The tart sweetness of the agrodolce is quite shocking at first, but you will soon appreciate the beautiful melange of flavours, especially with hits from the mint and pine nuts.

SERVES 4~6

2 cauliflower heads (about 1.5 kg),
   cut into florets
2–3 tablespoons extra-virgin olive oil
460 g farro, rinsed
½ cup pine nuts, toasted
1 cup mint leaves, roughly torn
1 cup basil leaves, roughly torn
40 g parmesan, shaved
sea salt and black pepper

AGRODOLCE DRESSING

2 teaspoons extra-virgin olive oil
1 small red onion, very finely sliced
310 ml (1¼ cups) red wine vinegar
115 g (½ cup) caster sugar
3 tablespoons dried currants
3 black peppercorns
1 bay leaf
1 juniper berry

SUBSTITUTES/OPTIONS

farro: pearl barley, spelt, freekeh or quinoa
For gluten free, use quinoa in place of farro
For vegans, omit parmesan

Preheat the oven to 200°C.

Place the cauliflower florets on a large baking tray, drizzle with 1–2 tablespoons of olive oil and season with salt. Roast for 25–30 minutes or until tender and golden.

Add the farro to a large saucepan of salted water and bring to the boil. Simmer for 30–35 minutes or until the farro grains are tender. Drain.

To make the agrodolce dressing, heat the olive oil in a saucepan, add the onion and sauté for 3–4 minutes until it is starting to caramelise. Add the vinegar and sugar, stirring to dissolve the sugar. Finally, add the currants, peppercorns, bay leaf and juniper berry and simmer for 15 minutes until the sauce has reduced and is thick and syrupy. Allow to cool.

To serve, combine the cauliflower with the farro and pour over the agrodolce dressing. Season with salt and pepper and toss to combine. Drizzle over some olive oil and scatter over the pine nuts, herbs and shaved parmesan.

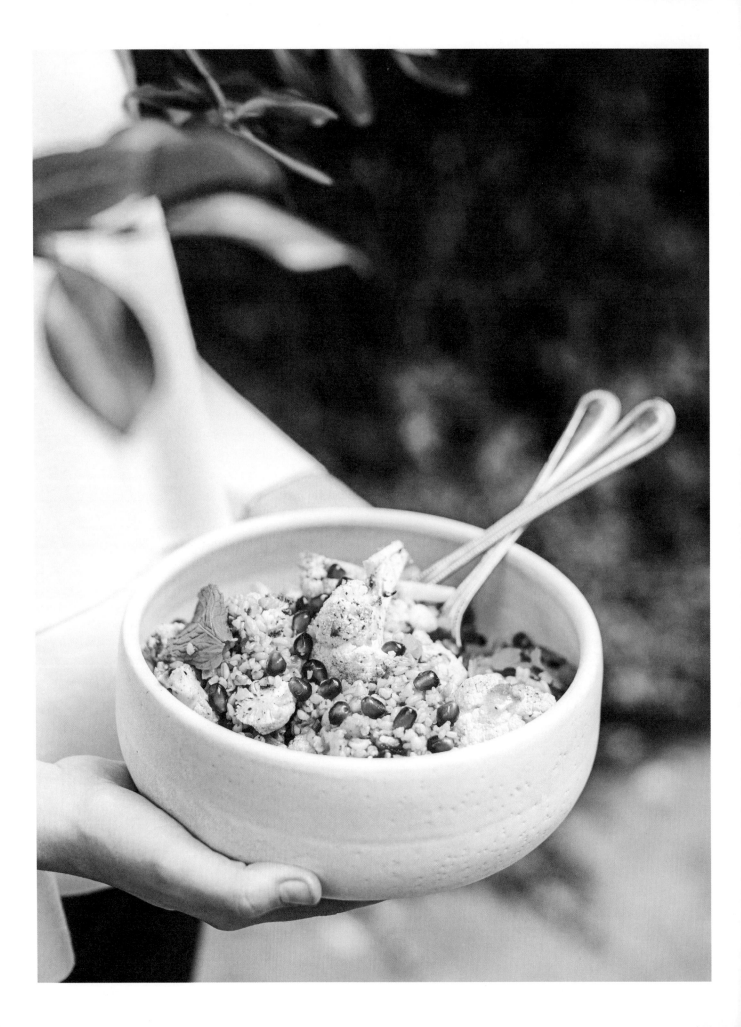

SUMAC-ROASTED CAULIFLOWER WITH SPICED FREEKEH AND POMEGRANATE

I'm always looking for new flavour accents to add to roasted cauliflower and sumac is one of my favourites. The sumac bush is native to the Middle East and its deep red berries are dried and ground to produce a vibrantly hued, tangy lemony powder. This simple cauliflower salad is full of surprises – sumac adds a lovely tart zest to the roasted cauliflower, while the pomegranate seeds deliver a surprise pop of flavour and colour to every mouthful.

VG | SERVES 4~6

2 cauliflower heads (about 1.5 kg),
   broken into small florets
4–5 tablespoons extra-virgin olive oil
2 teaspoons sumac
1 onion, finely diced
1 garlic clove, very finely chopped
1 teaspoon ground coriander
1 teaspoon ground cumin
300 g freekeh, rinsed
1 litre (4 cups) vegetable stock,
   broth or water
1 pomegranate, seeds extracted
½ cup mint leaves, torn
⅓ cup coriander leaves
⅓ cup basil leaves, torn
1 cup walnuts, toasted
2 tablespoons pomegranate molasses
sea salt and black pepper

SUBSTITUTES/OPTIONS

freekeh: farro, spelt, barley or quinoa
For gluten free, use quinoa in place
   of freekeh

Preheat the oven to 200°C.

Place the cauliflower florets on a large baking tray, coat in 2–3 tablespoons of olive oil and season with salt and pepper. Sprinkle over the sumac and roast for 20–25 minutes until golden.

Heat 1 tablespoon of oil in a saucepan over a medium heat, add the onion, garlic, coriander and cumin and sauté for 1–2 minutes until softened. Add the freekeh and stock, cover with a lid and cook for 20–25 minutes until the grains are tender. If more liquid is required, just add a bit of water.

Combine the freekeh with the cauliflower, pomegranate seeds and herbs. Dress with a little olive oil and season with salt and pepper. To serve, scatter over the toasted walnuts and drizzle with the pomegranate molasses.

HONEY-ROASTED BRUSSELS SPROUTS WITH QUINOA AND LENTIL PILAF

Brussels sprouts and honey may not be the most obvious pairing, but once you have tasted this spunky little food combo, you will not look back! The sweetness of the honey perfectly tempers the mustardy undertones of sprouts. Combined with this nourishing, spiced quinoa and lentil pilaf, this is a hearty salad bowl you will crave time and time again.

GF | SERVES 4~6

1 kg brussels sprouts, trimmed and halved
1–2 tablespoons extra-virgin olive oil
2 tablespoons honey
½ cup coriander leaves
½ cup mint leaves
⅓ cup hazelnuts, roasted and
　roughly chopped
sea salt and black pepper

QUINOA AND LENTIL PILAF

200 g green lentils, rinsed
2 tablespoons extra-virgin olive oil
1 onion, finely diced
1 garlic clove, finely chopped
2 teaspoons ground cumin
2 teaspoons ground coriander
½ teaspoon ground cinnamon
½ teaspoon ground turmeric
300 g red or white quinoa, rinsed
500 ml (2 cups) vegetable stock

OPTION

For vegans, use maple syrup in place
　of honey

Preheat the oven to 200°C.

Place the brussels sprouts on a large baking tray, drizzle over the olive oil and season with salt and pepper. Roast for 25–30 minutes, or until tender and golden. Remove from the oven and immediately drizzle over the honey.

For the quinoa and lentil pilaf, add the lentils to a large saucepan of boiling water with a big pinch of salt. Simmer over a medium heat for 20–25 minutes until soft. Drain. Heat the olive oil in a large saucepan over a medium heat, add the onion and garlic and sauté until soft. Add the spices and cook for about 30 seconds, until fragrant, then add the quinoa and stir to coat the grains in the spices. Pour over the vegetable stock, cover with a lid and cook for 20 minutes, or until the stock has been absorbed and the quinoa is translucent. Remove from the heat and leave the pilaf to sit for 5 minutes to enable the grains to fluff up. Stir in the lentils using a fork or chopsticks.

To serve, pile the pilaf onto a large platter, top with the honey-roasted brussels sprouts and scatter over the herbs and hazelnuts.

CHARGRILLED BRUSSELS SPROUTS AND KALE WITH CRUSHED BORLOTTI BEANS AND ZA'ATAR

This salad has so many dimensions of flavour – smoky charred brussels sprouts and crunchy roasted kale, sitting upon a bed of creamy smashed borlotti beans, topped with a healthy sprinkle of earthy za'atar. And a little tip: the crushed borlotti beans are lovely served on crostini as a starter or snack!

VG | GF | SERVES 4~6

700 g brussels sprouts, trimmed
3–4 tablespoons extra-virgin olive oil
1 bunch of kale leaves, washed and dried
    thoroughly, central stems removed
    and leaves torn
½ cup pitted black olives, halved
½ cup flat-leaf parsley leaves, finely chopped
2 tablespoons za'atar
sea salt

CRUSHED BORLOTTI BEANS

½ red onion, finely diced
3 teaspoons red wine vinegar
800 g cooked borlotti beans
    (about 3 cans), drained
2–3 tablespoons extra-virgin olive oil
sea salt and black pepper

SUBSTITUTES

borlotti beans: butterbeans, pinto beans,
    cannellini beans

Preheat the oven to 120°C.

To prepare the crushed borlotti beans, soak the red onion in a bowl of water with 1 teaspoon of the red wine vinegar for 10 minutes (this takes the 'bite' out of the onion). Drain. Add the borlotti beans to a large stainless steel bowl together with a huge pinch of salt and roughly crush using a potato masher, pestle or large fork. Add the olive oil and crush the beans some more to a coarse, 'smashed' texture (it doesn't have to be smooth). Add the remaining 2 teaspoons of red wine vinegar and the red onion and season with pepper and more salt (if required) to taste.

Depending on their size, cut each brussels sprout into 3–4 slices. Place in a large bowl, coat in 1–2 tablespoons of olive oil and season with salt.

Heat a griddle pan, large frying pan or barbecue to high. Add the brussels sprouts to the pan or barbecue and cook for 3 minutes on each side until tender and golden.

Place the kale leaves on a large baking tray, drizzle over 1 tablespoon of olive oil and massage it into the leaves. Roast for 20–25 minutes until the kale leaves are crispy. Remove from the oven and sprinkle lightly with salt.

To serve, spoon the crushed borlotti beans onto a large platter, top with the sprouts and kale and scatter over the black olives and parsley. Drizzle over a little olive oil and sprinkle over the za'atar to finish.

CUMIN-ROASTED SWEET POTATO WITH
HARISSA CHICKPEAS AND SPINACH

For me, harissa is an essential kitchen condiment. I add it to everything – roasted vegetables, omelettes, pasta, sandwiches. It adds an instant lift to just about any dish. While store-bought harissa usually does the job just fine (including in this recipe), you will be surprised by the deeper flavours of the homemade variety. I like to add some dried chipotle chillies to my harissa for that extra hit of smokiness. Any extra can be topped with a thin layer of oil and stored in the fridge for up to 14 days.

VG | GF | SERVES 4~6

5 medium–large sweet potatoes
   (about 1.75 kg), washed, unpeeled
   and cut into 1 cm cubes
2 teaspoons cumin seeds
2–3 tablespoons extra-virgin olive oil
2 red onions, finely sliced
500 g cooked chickpeas
   (about 2 cans), drained
3 tablespoons roughly chopped flat-leaf
   parsley leaves
¼ cup coriander leaves
2 cups baby spinach leaves
juice of ½ lemon
3 tablespoons flaked almonds, toasted
sea salt and black pepper

**SMOKY HARISSA
(MAKES ABOUT 270 G/1 CUP)**

1 large red capsicum, halved and deseeded
80 ml (⅓ cup) extra-virgin olive oil
2–3 dried chipotle chillies, soaked in
   boiling water for 30 minutes and drained
4 dry-packed sun-dried tomatoes,
   rehydrated in boiling water for
   30 minutes and drained
2 garlic cloves, chopped
1 teaspoon sea salt
¾ teaspoon ground coriander
½ teaspoon ground caraway
½ teaspoon ground cumin

SUBSTITUTES
sweet potato: carrot, eggplant, pumpkin

Preheat the oven to 200°C.

To make the harissa, begin by roasting your capsicum. Place the capsicum cut-side down on a large baking tray, drizzle with 1 tablespoon of olive oil and roast for 20–25 minutes, until the skin is charred slightly and the flesh is tender. Set aside to cool slightly, then peel away the skin. Wearing gloves, remove the seeds and stem from the soaked chipotle chillies. Place the capsicum and chipotle flesh, sun-dried tomatoes, garlic, salt, spices, remaining olive oil and 2 tablespoons of water in the bowl of a food processor and whizz together until you have a smooth, thick paste (add a little more water if it is too thick).

Place the sweet potato on a large baking tray, sprinkle over the cumin seeds, drizzle with 1–2 tablespoons of olive oil and season with salt and pepper. Combine well and roast in the oven for 20–25 minutes until tender.

Heat 1 tablespoon of olive oil in a large frying pan, add the onions with a pinch of salt and fry until soft, about 10 minutes. Add 4 tablespoons of harissa (or more depending on how hot you like it), the chickpeas and a pinch of salt and cook, stirring, for about 5 minutes until the chickpeas are well coated in the harissa and onions. Leave to cool.

Combine the sweet potato with the harissa chickpeas, herbs and baby spinach leaves. Add a squeeze of lemon juice and 2 tablespoons of harissa paste, season with salt and pepper and mix well. To serve, scatter over the almonds.

ISRAELI CHOPPED SALAD WITH TOMATOES, CUCUMBER, RADISH AND FETA

Over the years, I have had the good fortune to have many friends guide me in the art of an Israeli salad. The first was my good friend Gabi, who, in my old hood of Surry Hills, would nonchalantly whip up this fresh, colourful chopped tomato and cucumber salad with a dollop of cottage cheese. In Brooklyn, my new pals Leetal and Ron at NY Shuk furthered my love of this insanely simple salad, daring me to push the boundaries with lemon and olive oil. Everyone has their own version of Israeli salad but, learning from the best, this is my simple version.

GF | SERVES 4~6

3 large beefsteak tomatoes (about 1 kg),
   or other seasonal variety
4 small Lebanese cucumbers
   (about 400 g), trimmed
1 bunch of radishes (about 300 g), trimmed
1 red onion
3–4 Chinese shallots (see note page 32)
1 cup flat-leaf parsley leaves
½ cup mint leaves
½ cup coriander leaves
1 long green chilli, deseeded and
   finely chopped
juice of 1–2 lemons
160–200 ml extra-virgin olive oil
200 g sheep's milk feta, crumbled
sea salt and black pepper

If the tomatoes and cucumber have lots of seeds, cut them out and discard. Cut the tomatoes into roughly 5 mm cubes, followed by the cucumbers, radishes and red onion, making sure everything is about the same size. Chop the Chinese shallots, parsley, mint and coriander leaves as finely as possible. Place everything in a large mixing bowl and add in the chilli.

Now it is time to dress the salad with the lemon juice and olive oil. I encourage you to add these gradually – tasting, adding more and tasting again – until you achieve the acidity you like. Remember, this salad is designed to be very lemony.

To serve, season well with salt and pepper. Taste and add more lemon juice, if you like, and scatter over the crumbled feta.

CHARGRILLED EGGPLANT AND LENTILS WITH ROCKET, HERB TAHINI AND POMEGRANATE

Herb tahini is such a versatile addition to any home cook's repertoire. Add whichever herbs you have to hand. I have used parsley and mint for a lovely earthy addition, but you could also use coriander, oregano, basil, chives or a combination of all. This herb tahini is also a great dip for crackers or vegetable crudite. Eggplant and lentils is one of my all-time favourite vegetable–legume combos.

GF | SERVES 4~6

5 eggplants (2 kg), sliced into
   1-cm thick rounds
2–3 tablespoons extra-virgin olive oil
300 g brown lentils, rinsed
1 cup baby rocket leaves
½ cup mint leaves
½ cup coriander leaves
½ cup flat-leaf parsley leaves,
   roughly chopped
1 pomegranate, seeds extracted
sea salt and black pepper

HERB TAHINI

½ cup flat-leaf parsley leaves,
   roughly chopped
½ cup mint leaves, roughly torn
1 long green chilli, deseeded
1 small garlic clove, very finely chopped
135 g tahini paste
juice of ½ lemon
1 tablespoon honey
3 tablespoons extra-virgin olive oil
sea salt and black pepper

OPTION

For vegans, use maple syrup in place
   of honey

To make the herb tahini, place the herbs, chilli, garlic and tahini paste in the bowl of a food processor and whizz together until almost smooth. Add the lemon juice and honey and pulse together again. With the motor on, slowly drizzle in the olive oil and about 1–2 tablespoons of water until the tahini is the consistency of double cream. Season with salt and pepper.

Heat a griddle pan or barbecue to high. In a large bowl, coat the eggplant slices in the olive oil. Add the eggplant to the pan or barbecue and cook for about 2–3 minutes on each side until tender and charred. Remove and leave to cool slightly. When cool enough to handle, slice into finger-sized pieces and season well with salt and pepper.

Tip the lentils into a saucepan of water and bring to the boil. Add a big pinch of salt to the water and cook for 20–25 minutes, until the lentils are just tender. Drain.

Combine the eggplant with the lentils, rocket and herbs and fold through the herb tahini. Serve topped with pomegranate seeds.

EGGPLANT WITH HALOUMI, BEETROOT TZATZIKI AND YOGHURT FLATBREADS

One of my lasting memories of travelling in Turkey was the ubiquitous vegetable dishes smothered in yoghurt. This salad takes inspiration from the grandeur of creamy yoghurt-covered eggplant in Turkish cuisine, with a naturally vibrant beetroot-tinged tzatziki adding a colour-popping surprise. Serve with salty, chewy haloumi and these life-changing flatbreads and you'll have a new family favourite! This flatbread is simple to make and terrific cooked on a barbecue. As a time-saver, use pre-cooked whole beetroot.

SERVES 4~6

4 eggplants (about 1.6 kg)
4–5 tablespoons extra-virgin olive oil
350 g haloumi, cut into 5 mm thick slices
2 cups baby spinach leaves
1 cup walnuts, toasted and crushed
½ cup mint leaves, torn
½ cup coriander leaves
sea salt and black pepper
lemon wedges, to serve

YOGHURT FLATBREADS

240 g natural yoghurt
1 teaspoon sea salt
330 g self-raising flour,
    plus extra for dusting

BEETROOT TZATZIKI

2 small beetroot (about 250 g), peeled
1 teaspoon cumin seeds
1 small garlic clove
375 g Greek yoghurt
1 teaspoon honey
1 tablespoon chopped dill
2 tablespoons chopped mint leaves
juice of ½ lemon
2 teaspoons extra-virgin olive oil
sea salt and black pepper

SUBSTITUTES

eggplant: cauliflower
haloumi: feta (unfried)

Preheat the oven to 200°C.

For the flatbread, combine the yoghurt and salt in a large bowl and beat until smooth. Gradually add the flour, stirring, until a stiff dough forms. On a lightly floured surface, knead the dough, adding a little more flour if needed, until soft and slightly sticky. Place the dough in a lightly oiled bowl, cover with plastic wrap and leave to rest for 30 minutes.

For the beetroot tzatziki, place the beetroot in a small saucepan and cover with water. Bring to the boil, cover and simmer for 20–25 minutes or until the beetroot are tender. Drain and leave to cool, then finely grate. Toast the cumin seeds in a dry frying pan until fragrant, then add to a bowl along with the beetroot and remaining tzatziki ingredients. Season with salt and pepper, mix together well and transfer to the refrigerator to chill.

Peel strips of skin from the eggplants, from top to bottom, so it leaves a stripy pattern. Cut the eggplants into 2 cm cubes and arrange on a large baking tray in a single layer. Drizzle with 2–3 tablespoons of olive oil and roast for 25–30 minutes until soft and golden. Remove from the oven and season with salt.

Place the flatbread dough on a floured surface and divide it into six balls. Roll each ball into a 16 cm circle. Brush each side with olive oil and sprinkle with a little salt. Heat a frying pan over a medium–high heat, add the flatbreads to the pan one at a time and cook for 30–40 seconds on each side until they puff up and are golden in parts. Turn and repeat on the other side – don't overcook.

When almost ready to serve, brush each side of the haloumi with olive oil and cook on a griddle pan, large frying pan or barbecue. Cook for 1–2 minutes on each side until soft and golden.

To serve, spread the beetroot tzatziki generously over a serving platter. Combine the eggplant with the spinach, walnuts and herbs and spoon it over the tzatziki. Drizzle with olive oil and season with a pinch of salt and pepper. Serve with the haloumi, flatbread and some lemon wedges on the side, or roll everything up in the flatbread.

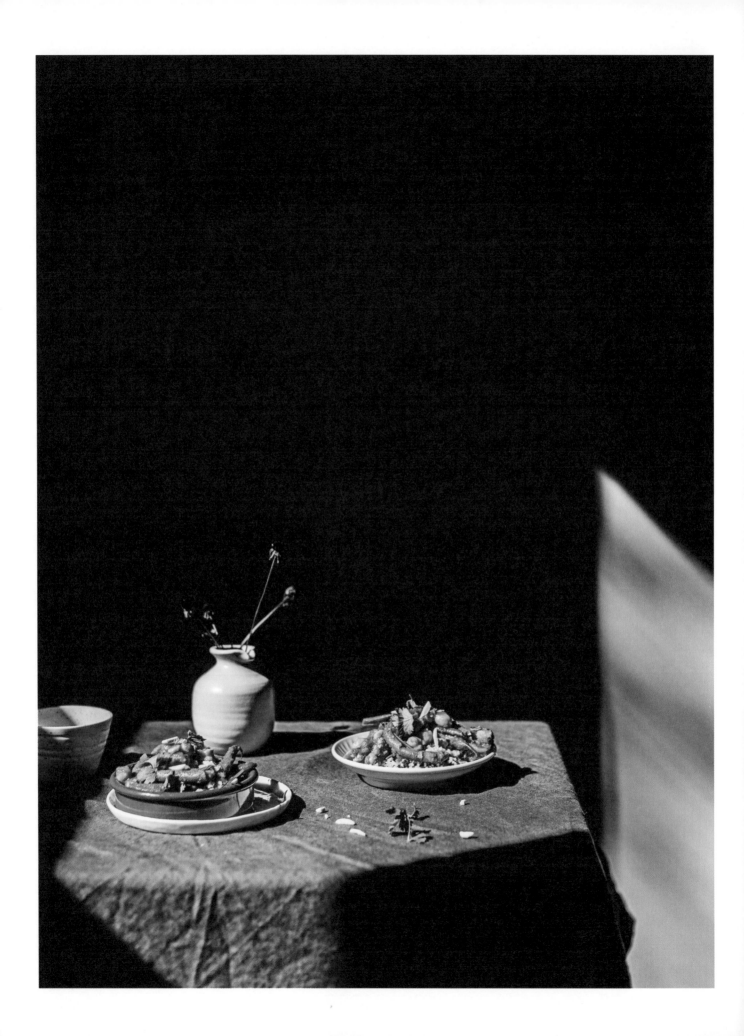

LEBANESE STEWED GREEN BEANS AND CHICKPEAS WITH SPINACH PILAF

If ever a salad embodied comfort, it would surely be this one. The simplest of ingredients – green beans, tomatoes and chickpeas – combine to create the most spectacular of flavours. This salad, inspired by Lebanese-style stewed beans, is even better the next day, so plan ahead if you can. The spinach and bulgur wheat pilaf is good enough to scoff all on its own!

VG | SERVES 4~6

1–2 tablespoons extra-virgin olive oil
1 tablespoon cumin seeds
1 teaspoon coriander seeds
1 onion, finely diced
2 garlic cloves, very finely chopped
3 tablespoons tomato paste
700 g green beans, trimmed
250 g cooked chickpeas
   (about 1 can), drained
400 g diced tomatoes (about 1 can)
½ cup coriander leaves, roughly chopped
3 tablespoons slivered almonds, toasted
sea salt and black pepper

SPINACH PILAF

1–2 tablespoons extra-virgin olive oil
1 small red onion, finely diced
1 garlic clove, very finely chopped
400 g bulgur wheat (cracked wheat)
750 ml (3 cups) vegetable stock or broth
3 cups baby spinach leaves, washed
   thoroughly and roughly chopped
sea salt

Heat the olive oil in a large casserole dish, add the cumin and coriander seeds and cook, stirring often, for about 1 minute or until the seeds are popping and fragrant. Add the onion and garlic, season well with salt and pepper and sauté until the onion is soft and golden, about 3–4 minutes. Add the tomato paste and cook for a further 2 minutes, then add the green beans, chickpeas, tomatoes and 80 ml (⅓ cup) of water. Bring to the boil, then reduce to a simmer, cover and cook for 45–60 minutes over a medium heat until the beans are very tender. Remove from the heat, season with salt and pepper to taste and leave to cool.

While the green beans are cooling, make the pilaf. In a large saucepan, heat the olive oil over a medium heat, add the onion and garlic and cook until the onion is soft and translucent, about 3–4 minutes. Add the bulgur wheat and stir to coat the grains in the hot oil. Pour over the vegetable stock and add a pinch of salt, then reduce the heat to low, cover with a lid and leave to cook for about 10 minutes. The pilaf is ready when all the liquid has been absorbed. When cooked, remove the lid and fold through the spinach leaves, then place a clean tea towel over the pan and replace the lid. Leave to stand and steam for 15 minutes (the residual heat will wilt the spinach).

To serve, combine the stewed beans and chickpeas with the pilaf. Sprinkle over the coriander and almonds to finish.

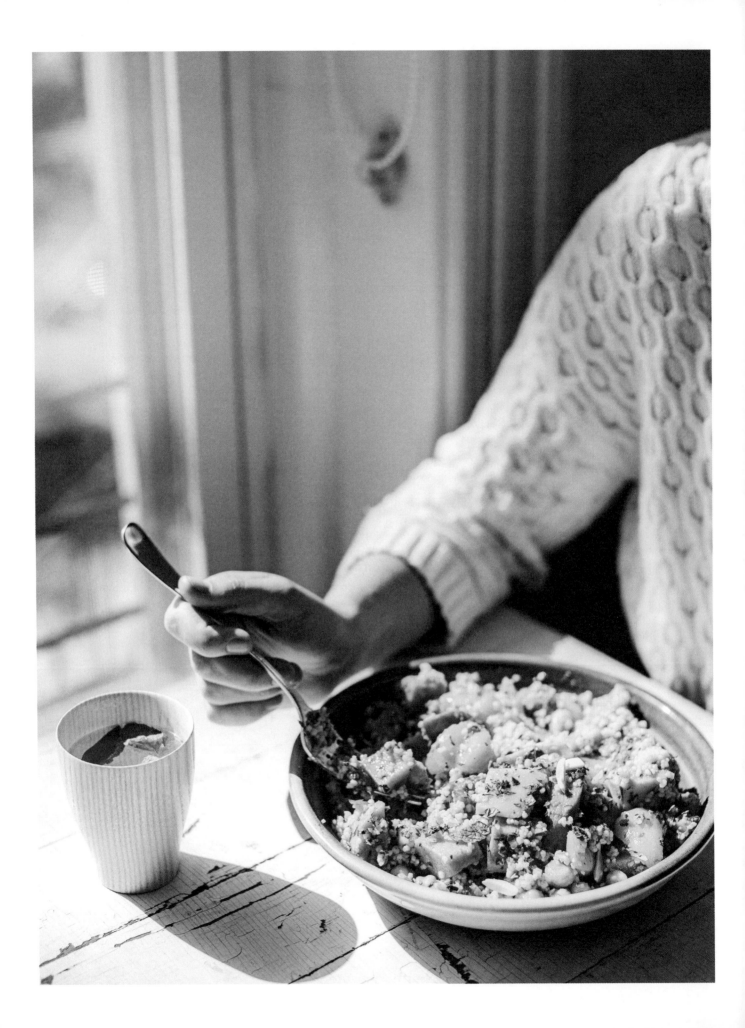

CHERMOULA-ROASTED ORANGE VEGETABLES
WITH CHICKPEAS AND COUSCOUS

Orange is the new black? In this salad, orange is definitely the hottest colour around. Butternut pumpkin, carrots, sweet potatoes and orange capsicums (though yellow are fine if you can't find orange!) are rubbed and roasted in chermoula, a heady spice rub commonly used in Tunisian, Moroccan, Libyan and Algerian cooking. Chermoula is classically served with couscous and chickpeas, as it is here in this salad. Make the chermoula in advance and store in the refrigerator for up to 5 days.

SERVES 4~6

185 g couscous
2 tablespoons extra-virgin olive oil
375 ml (1½ cups) boiling vegetable stock
    or broth
1 small butternut pumpkin (about 800 g),
    peeled and cut into 2 cm chunks
2 sweet potatoes (about 500 g), cut into
    2 cm chunks
3 carrots (about 350 g), peeled and
    cut into 2 cm chunks
3 orange capsicums, deseeded and
    cut into 2 cm chunks
2 tomatoes, roughly chopped
2 tablespoons honey
juice of ½ lemon
500 g cooked chickpeas
    (about 2 cans), drained
½ cup flat-leaf parsley leaves, finely chopped
½ cup coriander leaves, finely chopped
3 tablespoons slivered almonds, toasted
sea salt and black pepper

CHERMOULA

2 garlic cloves
2 teaspoons ground cumin
2 teaspoons paprika
½ teaspoon cayenne pepper
zest and juice of 1 lemon
1 teaspoon sea salt
3 tablespoons extra-virgin olive oil
½ cup flat-leaf parsley leaves, finely chopped
½ cup coriander leaves, finely chopped

OPTIONS

For gluten free, use quinoa or millet
    in place of couscous
For vegans, omit honey

To make the chermoula, using a mortar and pestle, pound together the garlic, cumin, paprika, cayenne, lemon zest, lemon juice and salt. Whisk in the olive oil until well combined. Stir in the parsley and coriander. Alternatively, you can use a food processor to mix together all the ingredients.

Preheat the oven to 120°C.

Put the couscous into a shallow bowl, along with 1 tablespoon of olive oil and stir through to coat the grains. Pour over the vegetable stock and stir well. Cover the bowl with plastic wrap and let stand for 10 minutes. Uncover, drizzle with the remaining olive oil and stir together, then cover with foil and heat in the oven for 5 minutes. Remove from the oven and fluff up the grains with a fork.

Increase the oven temperature to 200°C.

Place the pumpkin, sweet potato, carrots, capsicum and tomatoes on a large baking tray. Add enough of the chermoula to generously coat the vegetables (keeping the remainder aside for later) and rub it into the vegetables with your hands. Season with a pinch of salt and pepper and roast for 30–35 minutes until the vegetables are tender. Remove from the oven, immediately drizzle over the honey and squeeze over the lemon juice.

To serve, add the remaining chermoula to the vegetables and stir through. Combine the vegetables with the couscous, chickpeas and herbs. Season with salt and pepper and top with the almonds.

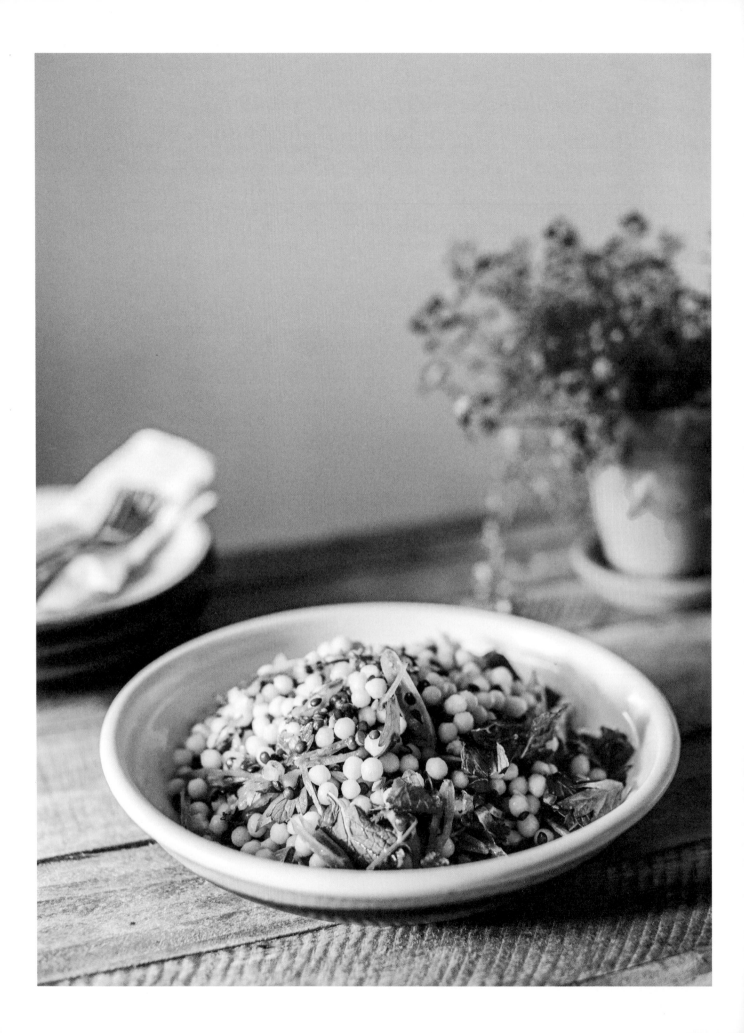

MOGHRABIEH WITH BLACK LENTILS AND SUGAR SNAP PEAS

Hailing from the Middle East, moghrabieh grains are like oversized couscous, made of semolina and formed into small, pasta-like balls. In Lebanon, moghrabieh, which is traditionally served with meat, is a feasting dish, a meal to share with family and friends. Here, I have taken the feasting to a new level, teaming hearty moghrabieh grains with fortifying black lentils, crispy sweet raw sugar snap peas and the most refreshing seasonal herbs.

VG | SERVES 4~6

400 g moghrabieh
1 garlic clove, very finely chopped
1.25 litres (5 cups) vegetable stock
100 g black lentils, rinsed
400 g sugar snap peas, trimmed and
   cut into very thin strips
½ cup flat-leaf parsley leaves,
   roughly chopped
½ cup mint leaves, roughly chopped
½ cup coriander leaves, roughly chopped
½ cup finely chopped Chinese shallots
   (see note page 32)
juice of 1–2 lemons
3–4 tablespoons extra-virgin olive oil
sea salt and black pepper

SUBSTITUTES

moghrabieh: pearl couscous, fregola
black lentils: brown, green or puy lentils
sugar snap peas: snow peas

Add the moghrabieh balls, chopped garlic and vegetable stock to a saucepan. Bring to the boil, then lower the heat to a rolling simmer and leave to cook for 20–25 minutes until the moghrabieh balls are al dente. Take off the heat, drain off the remaining liquid and run under cold water. Set aside to dry out a little.

In a medium saucepan, add the lentils and cover with plenty of cold water. Add a big pinch of sea salt. Bring to the boil, reduce the heat and cook for 20–25 minutes until just tender. Drain.

Using a very sharp knife, finely slice the sugar snap peas into razor-thin strips.

Combine the moghrabieh, lentils, pea strips and herbs. Dress with the lemon juice and olive oil and season well with salt and pepper. Taste and adjust the quantities of lemon juice and oil to achieve a balanced, tangy dressing.

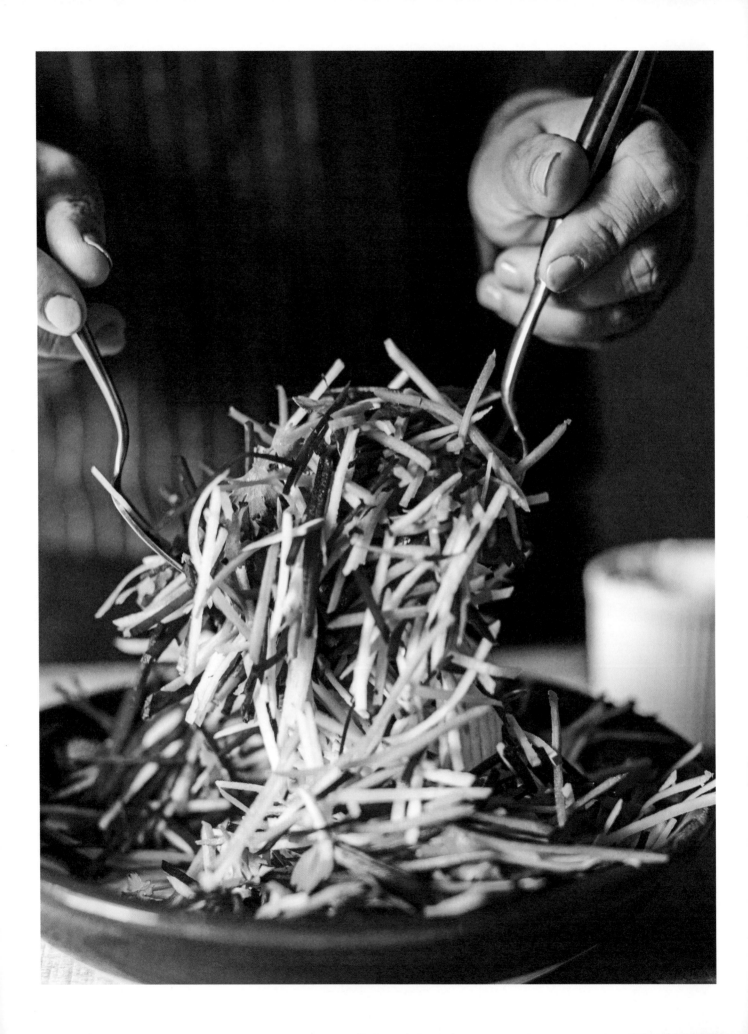

BEETROOT, KOHLRABI, CARROT AND APPLE SLAW WITH LABNEH

Labneh sounds exotic, but it is actually just strained yoghurt. As simple as it is to create, homemade labneh never fails to impress. You can get fancy and roll it into balls, cover in dukkah or za'atar and marinate in oil. You can add finely chopped radishes, carrots and shallots to create a flavoursome vegetable dip. Or you can just dollop it on top of salads, like I have here. In this salad, the creamy, slightly tart hum of the labneh completely enlivens this sweet and colourful raw party of beetroot, kohlrabi, carrot and apple.

GF | SERVES 4~6

1 kohlrabi (about 350 g), peeled
2 beetroot (about 350 g), peeled
2 carrots (about 350 g), peeled
2 apples (about 500 g), peeled
½ cup mint leaves
½ cup coriander leaves
½ cup flat-leaf parsley leaves
3 tablespoons pumpkin seeds, toasted

LABNEH

500 g Greek yoghurt
1 garlic clove, grated
sea salt and black pepper

SHERRY VINEGAR DRESSING

juice of ½ lemon
2 tablespoons extra-virgin olive oil
2 tablespoons sherry vinegar
2 teaspoons caster sugar
sea salt

SUBSTITUTE

kohlrabi: zucchini

Labneh needs making a day before you want to serve it and keeps in the fridge for 5 days, or longer if marinated. To make it, line a colander or sieve with a piece of muslin or a thin cotton sheet. Combine the yoghurt and garlic together with a pinch of salt and pepper, spoon it into the cloth and secure tightly with an elastic band or tie. Give the bundle a good squeeze over the sink, then put it back into the colander. Sit the colander over a shallow plate or bowl and leave it in the fridge for at least 24 hours. During this time, the yoghurt will lose its excess moisture, leaving a firmer mixture a bit like cream cheese. If you can, squeeze out any excess liquid from time to time to help this firming process.

To make the dressing, combine the lemon juice, olive oil, sherry vinegar, sugar and a pinch of sea salt in a small saucepan. Bring to a simmer and stir until the sugar and salt have fully dissolved. Set aside.

Using a mandoline, food processor or box grater, shave or grate the vegetables and apple into thin strips (leaving the apple for last as it will brown).

Place the shredded fruit and vegetables in a large bowl and immediately drizzle over the warm dressing. Add the herbs, season with salt and pepper and gently toss the salad with your hands. To serve, dot with big balls or spoonfuls of labneh and sprinkle over the pumpkin seeds.

LENTILS, LEEKS, RICE AND CARAMELISED ONIONS WITH LEMON–TOMATO OKRA

When I was about 15, I started to experiment in the kitchen with foods from other cultures. One of the first meals I cooked for myself was a mujaddara recipe from my Australian Women's Weekly *Middle Eastern cookbook. I remember being entranced by the flavours of this very simple Lebanese dish of rice, lentils and caramelised onions. This is my version, with leeks and a lemon-laced okra. The lemon in the okra serves a double purpose – it adds a lovely zestiness and also, as I learned from my good friend Sneh Roy from the blog Cook Republic, it also eliminates some of okra's sliminess!*

VG | GF | SERVES 4~6

3 tablespoons extra-virgin olive oil
3 leeks, white and light green parts only,
  finely sliced and washed
1 garlic clove, finely chopped
400 g basmati rice, rinsed
2 teaspoons ground cumin
1 teaspoon ground allspice
½ teaspoon cayenne pepper
200 g brown lentils, rinsed
2 bay leaves
2 cinnamon sticks
1.5 litres (6 cups) vegetable stock
6 onions, halved and finely sliced
1 teaspoon caster sugar
1 cup coriander leaves
sea salt and black pepper

LEMON–TOMATO OKRA

1 tablespoon extra-virgin olive oil
2 garlic cloves, finely chopped
1 teaspoon ground cumin
400 g okra, washed and trimmed
4 roma tomatoes (about 500 g),
  cut into 1 cm dice
juice of 1 lemon
sea salt

Heat 2 tablespoons of olive oil in a casserole dish or large saucepan over a medium heat. Add the leeks, season with a pinch of salt and sauté for 7–8 minutes until soft and golden. Add the garlic and rice and cook for 2 minutes, then stir in the cumin, allspice and cayenne pepper and cook for 30 seconds. Add the lentils, bay leaves and cinnamon sticks and stir in the vegetable stock. Bring to a steady simmer, cover and cook for 20 minutes or so, until the rice and lentils are both cooked and the liquid has been absorbed. Remove the lid, discard the bay leaves and cinnamon stick and leave to cool.

Meanwhile, heat 1 tablespoon of olive oil in a frying pan and add the onions, sugar and a big pinch of salt. Sauté over a medium heat for 15–20 minutes, until the onions are golden and caramelised.

For the lemon–tomato okra, heat the olive oil in a large frying pan over a high heat, add the garlic and cumin and fry for 10 seconds until fragrant. Add the okra with a pinch of salt and fry for 5 minutes, until tender and golden. Stir in the tomatoes along with 2 tablespoons of water and cook for another 5 minutes until the tomatoes are just soft. Take off the heat and squeeze in the lemon juice.

To serve, transfer the rice and lentil mixture onto a large serving platter, spoon over the lemon okra and top with the caramelised onions. Scatter over the coriander leaves.

TO ASIA, WITH LOVE

Asian fare is my comfort food. Though I was born and raised in Sydney, I am Chinese deep in my heart. The flavours of my childhood still transport me to my happy place. When I am homesick or need a big hit of flavour, I always turn to dumplings, a rambling bowl of noodles, braised shiitake mushrooms with tofu or stir-fried broccoli. Now, Asian salads are my favourite dishes to make, affording me the ultimate opportunity to flex my multi-cultural muscle — I can experiment with a deep umami dressing, splash out with something spicy or adorned with peanuts, pursue a dish with a tropical twist, or opt for a finish that is a little sweet and a little savoury. In an Asian salad, there is heart, home and love.

BRUSSELS SPROUTS WITH STIR-FRIED LOTUS ROOT, BLACK FUNGUS, FIVE-SPICE TOFU AND HOISIN–SESAME SAUCE

Even if I'm on the other side of the world, the bustle of the local Chinatown is where I feel closest to my family. When I'm in a foreign city, I habitually seek out rustic looking Chinese restaurants to listen to the locals speak Cantonese and to take in the distinctive Chinatown aromas that are somehow the same, no matter where you are! This salad is inspired by the unabashed flavours of Cantonese cuisine.

VG | SERVES 4~6

700 g brussels sprouts, trimmed and halved
2–3 tablespoons extra-virgin olive oil
75 g black wood ear fungus
400 g frozen lotus root, defrosted for
    30 minutes
220 g five-spice tofu (about 1 packet),
    finely sliced into thin strips
3 tablespoons finely sliced Chinese shallots
    (see note page 32)
3 tablespoons roughly chopped
    coriander leaves
1 tablespoon white sesame seeds, toasted
1 tablespoon black sesame seeds
3 tablespoons crispy fried shallots
sea salt and black pepper

HOISIN–SESAME SAUCE

3 tablespoons hoisin sauce
3 tablespoons tahini paste
1 tablespoon sesame oil
1 tablespoon rice bran oil (or other
    neutral oil)
1 garlic clove, grated
sea salt and black pepper

SUBSTITUTES

frozen lotus root: fresh lotus root,
    water chestnuts, bamboo shoots
black fungus: shiitake mushrooms
five-spice tofu: pan-fried firm tofu

Preheat the oven to 200°C.

Place the halved brussels sprouts on a large baking tray, drizzle with 1–2 tablespoons of olive oil and season well with salt and pepper. Roast the brussels sprouts for 25–30 minutes until slightly charred and tender.

To make the sauce, combine the hoisin sauce and tahini paste, then slowly add 3 tablespoons of water, stirring as you go. Add the sesame oil, rice bran oil and garlic and stir together until well combined. Season well with salt and pepper.

Soak the black fungus in hot water for 15 minutes. Drain and dry with a tea towel and tear the larger pieces in half. Carefully pick through the fungus to remove any hard stems or debris. Heat 1 tablespoon of olive oil in a large frying pan or wok, add the lotus root (careful, the oil will spit!) and fry for 3–4 minutes until mostly defrosted. Add the black fungus and a big pinch of salt and stir-fry until the lotus root is cooked through and has taken on some colour, about 5 minutes. You will hear the fungus crackle and pop in the pan, which is normal.

Combine the brussels sprouts with the lotus root, black fungus, tofu and herbs. Add the sauce and toss well. Scatter over the sesame seeds and top with the crispy fried shallots.

THAI CARROT AND PEANUT SALAD

For me, home is where I am close to a great local Thai eatery. Having left Sydney, home to so many wonderful, inexpensive Thai restaurants, one of my first missions in my new neighbourhood of Carroll Gardens in Brooklyn was to find my local Thai joint. And just a few blocks away, I found it. One day, over lunch with my kids, I tasted a smashing peanut sauce that inspired me to create this salad. This dish features raw shredded carrot, crisp bean sprouts and tofu, escorted by a punchy peanut sauce.

GF | SERVES 4~6

800 g firm tofu, cut into 1 cm thick slices
1 tablespoon olive oil
10 small carrots (about 1 kg), peeled
180 g bean sprouts
1 kaffir lime leaf, very finely sliced
3 cups Asian herb leaves (Thai basil,
   coriander, Chinese shallots, Vietnamese
   mint or perilla)
½ cup roasted peanuts, roughly chopped
sea salt and black pepper

SPICY PEANUT SAUCE

120 g peanut butter
3 cm piece of ginger, peeled and grated
3 tablespoons honey
½ teaspoon caster sugar
1 tablespoon tamari
2 tablespoons vegetable oil
1 tablespoon sesame oil
2 tablespoons rice wine vinegar
juice of 1 lime
small pinch of chilli flakes
sea salt

To make the spicy peanut sauce, combine all the ingredients in the bowl of a food processor and whizz together to form a creamy sauce. Alternatively, combine the ingredients together in a small bowl with a whisk. Add a splash of water if it is too thick – you want the consistency of pouring cream. Season with salt to taste.

Coat the tofu slices in the olive oil and season well with salt and pepper. Heat a large frying pan over a medium heat, add the tofu slices and fry for 3–4 minutes on each side until golden. Leave to cool completely, then slice the tofu into thin strips.

Using a mandoline, grater attachment on your food processor or box grater, grate the carrots into thin strips.

Combine the carrots with the bean sprouts, tofu strips, kaffir lime leaf and herbs and toss well. Add the peanut sauce and toss again. To serve, top with the peanuts.

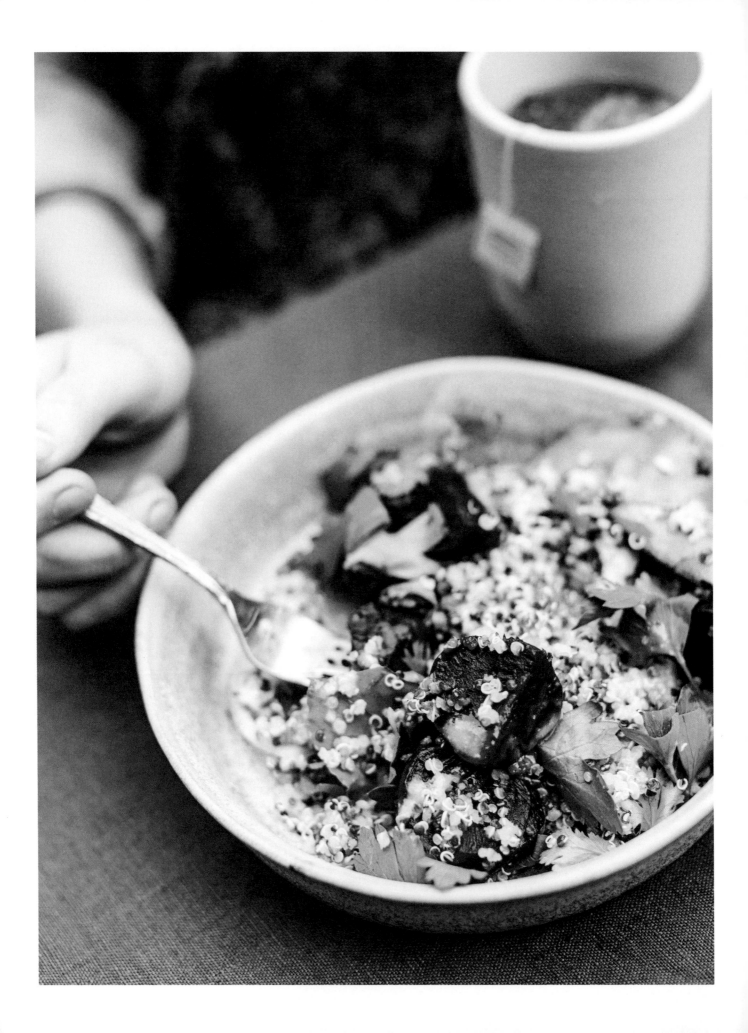

ROASTED BEETROOT WITH QUINOA, ESCHALOTS AND ORANGE MISO

Miso is such a wonderful pantry staple. And it is surprisingly versatile in salad making. In this salad, the umami goodness of the slightly sweet, slightly citrus orange miso really brings out the earthy worldliness of the beetroot. Use whatever beetroot are in season, whether they be regular crimsons, goldens, target beetroot or baby varieties. If your beetroot have lovely green tops, reserve them for your salad.

VG | GF | SERVES 4~6

8 small beetroot (about 1 kg), peeled and cut into 2 cm cubes, leaves reserved and torn
4 eschalots (see note page 32), peeled and finely sliced
2 tablespoons extra-virgin olive oil
400 g white or red quinoa, rinsed
750 ml (3 cups) vegetable stock, broth or water
3 tablespoons roughly chopped flat-leaf parsley leaves
½ cup coriander leaves
½ cup slivered almonds, toasted (optional)
sea salt and black pepper

ORANGE-MISO DRESSING

3 tablespoons miso paste
1 tablespoon sesame oil
1 garlic clove, grated
2.5 cm piece of ginger, peeled and grated
1 tablespoon maple syrup
125 ml (½ cup) freshly squeezed orange juice

SUBSTITUTE

beetroot leaves: baby rocket leaves

Preheat the oven to 200°C.

Combine the beetroot with the eschalots and spread over a large baking tray. Drizzle over the olive oil and season with salt and pepper. Roast for 25–30 minutes until the beetroot are tender.

Placed the rinsed quinoa in a large saucepan and add the vegetable stock and a big pinch of salt. Bring to the boil, then lower the heat and simmer for 15–20 minutes until the quinoa is tender and translucent. When cooked, turn off the heat and leave the quinoa to sit uncovered in the pan for 10 minutes, to allow the grains to separate and dry out.

To make the dressing, whisk together all the ingredients until well combined.

Combine the beetroot, beetroot leaves, eschalots, quinoa and herbs with the dressing and toss well. To serve, top with the almonds, if using.

ROASTED CARROTS WITH GREEN BEANS, MUNG BEANS AND COCONUT DUKKAH

It is so satisfying to make a batch of dukkah. So expensive to buy, but so simple to make at home, I always have some on hand to top roasted vegetables, salads or even sandwiches. This coconut dukkah was the result of a little kitchen experiment, when I was craving coconut. It adds a tropical, South-East Asian feel to the salad. This recipe makes a generous amount of coconut dukkah, more than you will need for this recipe – keep extra in the pantry or give it as a gift (if you don't want extra, simply halve the recipe).

VG | GF | SERVES 4~6

1 red onion, finely sliced
4–5 tablespoons extra-virgin olive oil
10 carrots (about 1.5 kg), sliced diagonally
300 g dried mung beans
250 g green beans, trimmed
½ cup coriander leaves
¼ cup flat-leaf parsley leaves
3 tablespoons finely sliced Chinese shallots
   (see note page 32)
juice of ½ lemon
sea salt and black pepper

COCONUT DUKKAH (MAKES 1 CUP)

4 white peppercorns
2 tablespoons coriander seeds
2 tablespoons cumin seeds
½ cup almonds or shelled pistachios, toasted
45 g (½ cup) desiccated coconut, toasted
2 tablespoons white sesame seeds, toasted
1 tablespoon black sesame seeds
1 tablespoon nigella seeds
1 teaspoon sea salt

SUBSTITUTE

desiccated coconut: fresh coconut

Preheat the oven to 200°C.

To make the coconut dukkah, place a frying pan over a medium heat and toast the peppercorns and the coriander and cumin seeds until fragrant and popping, about 60 seconds. Add to a mortar and pound with a pestle to a coarse powder, then add the nuts and pound again until chunky. Mix through the coconut, sesame seeds, nigella seeds and salt.

Coat the red onion slices in 2 teaspoons of olive oil and set aside. Place the carrots on a large baking tray, coat in 1–2 tablespoons of olive oil, season with salt and pepper and place in the oven to roast. After 20 minutes, add the sliced red onion to the baking tray and roast for a further 10 minutes or until the carrots and onion are both tender and golden.

Bring a saucepan of salted water to the boil, add the mung beans and simmer for 25–30 minutes until tender. Drain.

In a large frying pan, add 1 tablespoon of olive oil and fry the green beans until just tender and starting to colour. Remove from the pan.

Combine the carrots, mung beans, green beans, herbs, a drizzle of olive oil and a good squeeze of lemon juice and season with salt and pepper to taste. Scatter over the coconut dukkah and serve.

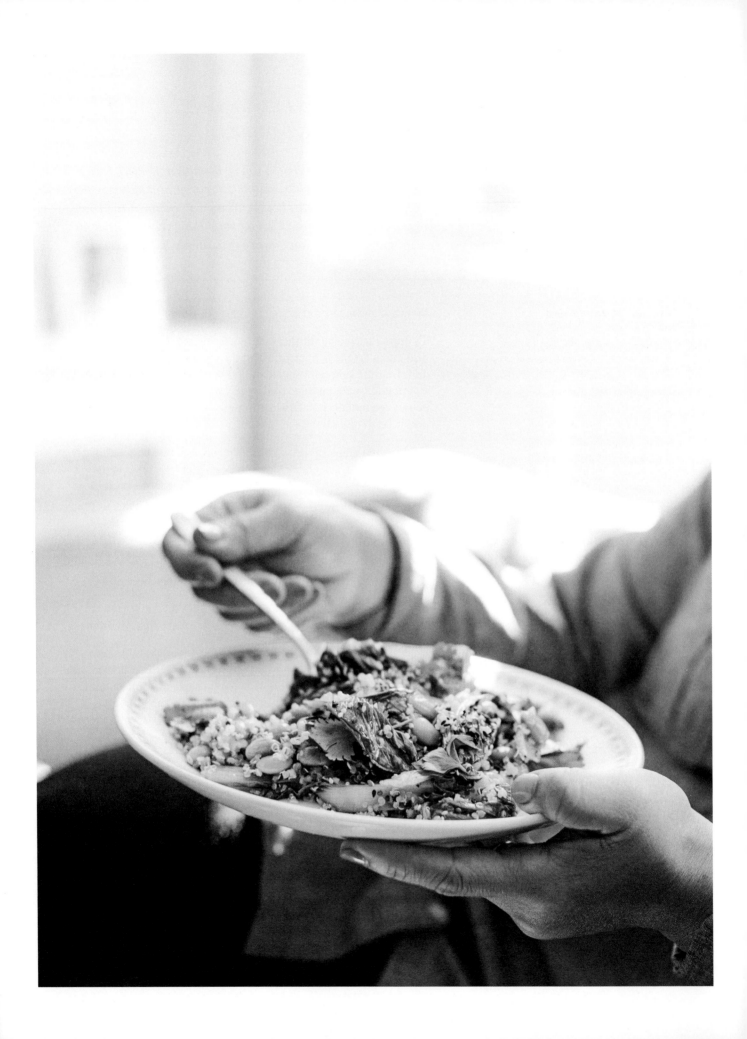

EDAMAME BEANS WITH BABY BOK CHOY, QUINOA AND HONEY–GINGER DRESSING

This salad is inspired by an afternoon of cooking with photographer and author Karen Mordechai at the incomparable Sunday Suppers in Williamsburg, Brooklyn. Karen kindly invited me to her stunning community kitchen to cook a salad. I brought along some local Greenmarket finds and she raided her pantry. That day, we cooked an Asian-inspired salad, similar to this dish. Feel free to use your favourite Asian greens and, if you can find them, definitely use fresh soy beans.

GF | SERVES 4~6

1 teaspoon vegetable stock powder
400 g white or red quinoa, rinsed
1 teaspoon sesame oil
1 tablespoon extra-virgin olive oil
400 g frozen podded edamame beans
4–5 bunches of baby bok choy,
  leaves separated
2 tablespoons white sesame seeds, toasted
2 tablespoons black sesame seeds
½ cup coriander leaves
sea salt and white pepper

HONEY–GINGER DRESSING

2.5 cm piece of ginger, peeled
1 small garlic clove
1 tablespoon honey
1 tablespoon rice wine vinegar
2 tablespoons mirin
1 tablespoon sesame oil
3 tablespoons extra-virgin olive oil
sea salt and white pepper

SUBSTITUTES

baby bok choy: choy sum, Chinese
  broccoli, tatsoi

To make the dressing, using a Microplane or the finest setting on a box grater, finely grate the ginger and garlic. Place in a bowl with the honey, vinegar, mirin and oils and whisk together. Add a pinch of salt, taste and adjust the seasoning if required.

Add the stock powder, quinoa, a pinch of salt and 750 ml (3 cups) of water to a saucepan. Bring to the boil, then reduce to a simmer and cook for 15–20 minutes, or until all the liquid has been absorbed and the quinoa is translucent. Turn the heat off and leave the quinoa to sit, uncovered, for 10 minutes to allow the grains to separate and dry out.

Heat the sesame and olive oils in a large frying pan or wok. Add the edamame beans with a pinch of salt and a splash of water and stir-fry for 3–4 minutes, then throw in the bok choy leaves and stir-fry for a further minute, until the leaves are just wilted but still bright green and the edamame are tender.

Combine the edamame beans and bok choy with the quinoa and season with salt and white pepper. Add the honey–ginger dressing and toss well. To serve, scatter over the sesame seeds and coriander leaves.

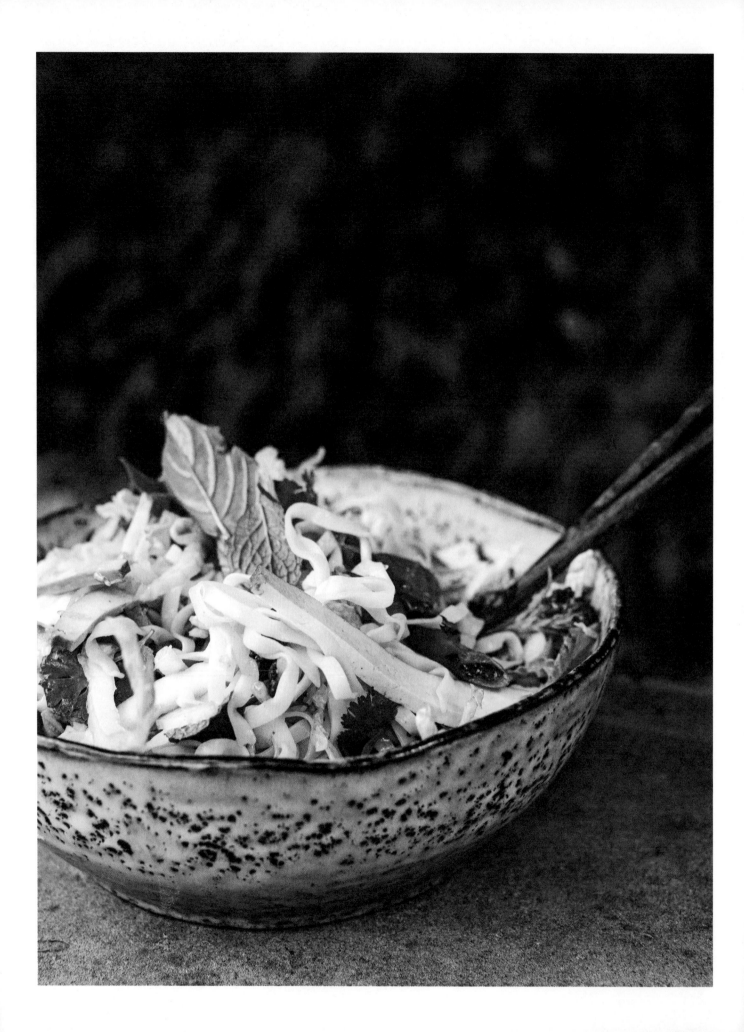

PHO NOODLE SALAD WITH TOFU, WOMBOK AND BROCCOLINI

When we lived in Sydney, my family would often head over to the neighbourhood of Marrickville to have a bowl of pho. Well, for the others, not me! I would covetously sit by and literally salivate over the intoxicating bouquet of cinnamon, cloves, ginger and star anise! Having been a vegetarian for over twenty years, pho noodle soup is really one of the only meat dishes that tempts me. So here, I bring my flesh-free pho dreams to life in an irresistible noodle salad.

VG | GF | SERVES 4~6

350 g thick dried rice noodles
1 tablespoon extra-virgin olive oil
400 g broccolini, trimmed and sliced
    diagonally into 2.5 cm pieces
120 g wombok cabbage, finely sliced
220 g five-spice tofu (about 1 packet),
    finely sliced into thin strips
180 g bean sprouts
1 cup Asian herb leaves (Thai basil,
    coriander, Chinese shallots, Vietnamese
    mint or perilla)
1 long red chilli, finely chopped (optional)
1 lime, cut into wedges
sea salt and white pepper

PHO DRESSING

2 onions, peeled and halved
7 cm piece of ginger, peeled and halved
    lengthways
1 cinnamon stick
5 white peppercorns
3 star anise
3 whole cloves
1 teaspoon coriander seeds
1.5 litres (6 cups) vegetable stock or water
1 tablespoon tamari
6 carrots, peeled and coarsely chopped
3 dried shiitake mushrooms
3 tablespoons extra-virgin olive oil
sea salt

SUBSTITUTES

broccolini: broccoli
wombok: green cabbage

To make the dressing, place the onions and ginger pieces directly on the flame of a gas hob or under a very hot grill until they are slightly blackened all over. Heat a large saucepan over a medium–low heat. Add the cinnamon, peppercorns, star anise, cloves and coriander seeds and toast, stirring to prevent burning, for 30 seconds until aromatic. Add the vegetable stock, tamari, carrots, mushrooms, charred onion and ginger to the pan and bring to the boil, then reduce the heat to low and simmer, uncovered, for 60–80 minutes until reduced by a third. Strain. Season with salt to taste and whisk in the olive oil.

Bring a large saucepan of salted water to the boil, add the rice noodles and cook for 6–8 minutes until tender. Drain and refresh under cold running water.

In a frying pan, add the olive oil and pan-fry the broccolini for about 5 minutes, until just tender and lightly charred.

Combine the noodles, wombok, broccolini, tofu, bean sprouts and herbs and pour over some of the dressing. Mix together well, making sure everything is coated in the dressing and season with salt and white pepper. Serve topped with chopped chilli (if you like) and lime wedges.

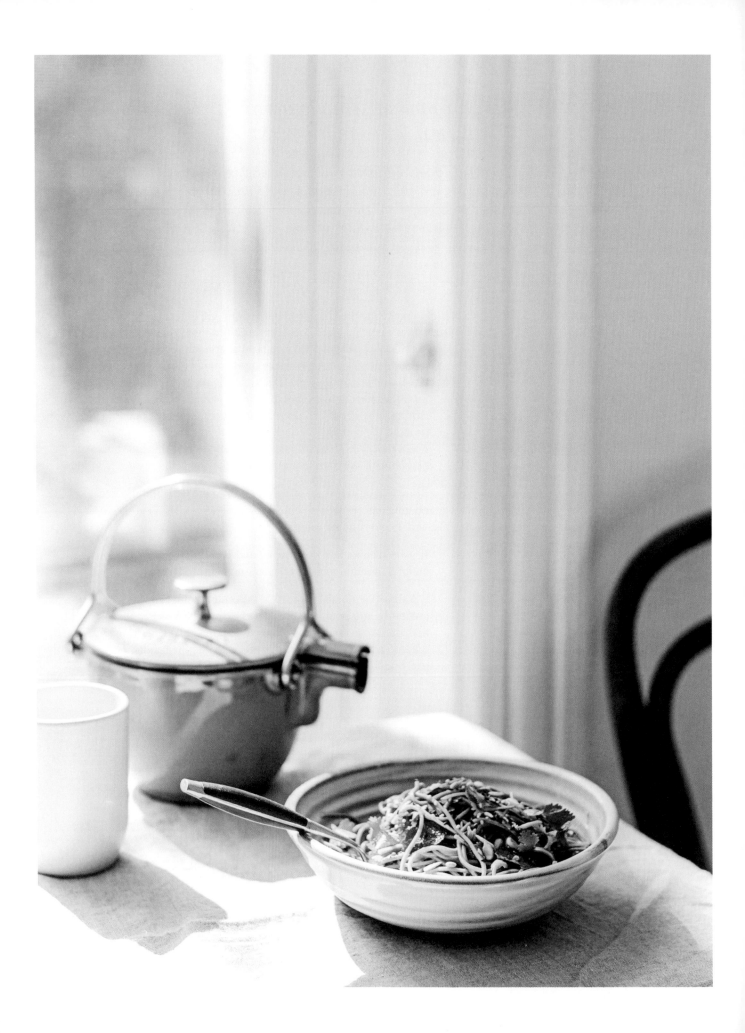

SEEDY SOBA NOODLES WITH ASIAN HERBS

Soba, with its robust texture and hearty buckwheat flavour, is the consummate salad noodle. While I religiously enjoy most of my salads at room temperature, I like my soba chilled. This salad was created for the love of texture: smooth, silky cold noodles loaded up with whatever seeds you can think of and a host of Asian herbs that really take centre stage.

SERVES 4~6

500 g soba noodles
1–2 tablespoons olive oil
1 cup coriander leaves
½ cup Thai basil or regular basil leaves
½ cup Vietnamese mint or regular
  mint leaves
½ cup finely chopped Chinese shallots
  (see note page 32)
1 cup sunflower seeds, toasted
1 cup pumpkin seeds, toasted
½ cup white sesame seeds, toasted
½ cup black sesame seeds
3 tablespoons nigella seeds
sea salt and white pepper

SWEET GINGER DRESSING

3 cm piece of ginger, peeled and grated
1 garlic clove, grated
2 tablespoons honey
3 tablespoons extra-virgin olive oil
2 tablespoons sesame oil
1 tablespoon cider vinegar
sea salt and white pepper

SUBSTITUTES

soba noodles: mung bean vermicelli,
  rice noodles

Bring a large pot of salted water to the boil, add the soba noodles and cook for 3–4 minutes, stirring constantly to prevent sticking, until just tender. Drain and refresh under cold running water. Place the noodles in the fridge for at least 1 hour to chill.

To make the dressing, mix together the ginger and garlic in a small bowl. Add the remaining ingredients and whisk everything together. Season with salt and white pepper.

To serve, place the chilled noodles in a large bowl and loosen them up with the olive oil (any variety is okay). Roughly chop or tear the herb leaves and add them to the bowl with the Chinese shallots, seeds and dressing. Toss gently to combine and season with salt and white pepper.

LEMONGRASS TOFU WITH ASIAN GREENS AND MUNG BEAN VERMICELLI

I have a strong affection for lemongrass and not only because of its tropical, citrus scent and its potent medicinal qualities. Lemongrass also reminds me of the suburban Sydney house where I grew up. We always had lemongrass growing in our backyard and later, when we lived in Surry Hills, my mother supplied lemongrass cuttings that grew robustly in our community verge garden. This salad is full of lemongrass goodness and fond memories.

VG | SERVES 4~6

600 g firm tofu, cut into 2 cm cubes
200 g mung bean vermicelli, soaked
    in warm water for 10 minutes
2–3 tablespoons vegetable oil
1 small onion, halved and finely sliced
400 g mixed Asian greens (bok choy,
    choy sum and Chinese broccoli),
    cut into 5 cm pieces
2 cups Asian herb leaves (Thai basil,
    coriander, Chinese shallots, Vietnamese
    mint or perilla), finely sliced
1–2 tablespoons extra-virgin olive oil
½ cup roasted peanuts, roughly chopped
sea salt and white pepper

LEMONGRASS MARINADE

4 lemongrass stalks, white parts only,
    very finely chopped
1 garlic clove, very finely chopped
3 tablespoons kecap manis
1 tablespoon soy sauce
½ teaspoon red chilli flakes
1 teaspoon ground turmeric
1 teaspoon caster sugar
pinch of sea salt

OPTION

For gluten free, use tamari in place
    of soy sauce

For the lemongrass marinade, combine all the ingredients in a bowl and whisk together. The marinade can be made the day before and kept in the fridge until ready to use.

Add the tofu cubes to the marinade, turning to coat evenly, and leave to marinate in the fridge for at least 30 minutes.

When ready to cook, put the vermicelli in a large bowl and soak in warm water for 10 minutes. Drain, return to the bowl and season with a big pinch of salt, then pour over enough boiling water to cover and leave for 10–20 seconds to soften fully. Drain immediately and rinse under cold water.

In a large frying pan, heat the vegetable oil and add the onion. Stir-fry the onion for 3–4 minutes until soft, then remove from the pan and set aside. Add the tofu to the pan along with the marinade and cook, moving the tofu pieces around with chopsticks or tongs, until golden brown all over. Return the onion to the pan along with the Asian greens and stir-fry for a further 1–2 minutes, until the greens are wilted.

Combine the tofu and greens with the mung bean vermicelli and herbs and drizzle over the olive oil. Toss together well, season with salt and white pepper and scatter over the peanuts to serve.

THIS IS AUSTRALIA

Modern Australia is a vibrant mix of cultures from all over the globe. Indeed, this interweaving of influences and experiences is precisely what makes Australia 'the lucky country'. The Australian table is where food from many different backgrounds and traditions is welcomed and celebrated. Aussie cuisine is light, fresh and always innovative, inspired by our cosmopolitan cities, golden beaches, rugged bush and blended history. The salads inspired by the Australia of today can also be identified as Modern Asian, Asian Fusion, Mediterranean-Inspired, New Middle-Eastern, Contemporary British or Nouveau French. This is culinary pluralism at its best — this is Australia.

TARATOR CAULIFLOWER WITH RAINBOW CHARD
AND BULGUR WHEAT

My good friend Elham Abi-Ghanem is a neighbourhood treasure. Elham was born in Senegal, of Lebanese descent, and now resides in inner city Sydney where she shares her vast knowledge and love of food with the kids at Bourke Street Public School (where she has volunteered and run the canteen for over 20 years). I have been lucky enough to learn a lot from Elham – she taught me all about this lemony Lebanese tarator, which I have classically teamed with cauliflower and chard (including the stalks!).

VG | SERVES 4~6

1 large cauliflower head (about 1 kg),
   cut into florets
5–6 tablespoons extra-virgin olive oil
1 small onion, finely diced
1 garlic clove, finely chopped
200 g bulgur wheat (cracked wheat)
375 ml (1½ cups) vegetable stock
200 g rainbow chard, leaves and
   stalks separated
½ cup flat-leaf parsley leaves,
   roughly chopped
juice of ½ lemon
½ cup slivered almonds, toasted
sea salt and black pepper

TARATOR

270 g tahini paste
1 garlic clove, very finely chopped
juice of 1 large lemon, plus extra if necessary
3 tablespoons finely chopped flat-leaf
   parsley leaves
sea salt and black pepper

SUBSTITUTES/OPTIONS

rainbow chard: spinach, kale, cavolo nero
For gluten free, use quinoa in place of
   bulgur wheat

Preheat the oven to 200°C.

Make the tarator by mixing together the tahini, garlic and lemon juice. Gradually stir in 5 tablespoons of water, a little at a time, until you have a smooth, creamy sauce. You want the consistency of cream. Taste and add a little more lemon juice, if you like, then stir in the parsley and season with salt and lots of pepper.

Place the cauliflower florets on a large baking tray and pour over two-thirds of the tarator, keeping some aside for serving. Drizzle over 1–2 tablespoons of olive oil and mix everything well to coat. Season with salt and pepper and roast for 20–25 minutes until golden.

Heat 2 tablespoons of olive oil in a saucepan over a low heat, add the onion and sauté for 1 minute until softened. Add the garlic and bulgur wheat and stir well to coat the grains in the oil. Pour over the stock, cover with a lid, bring to a simmer and cook for 10 minutes, or until the stock has been absorbed and the grains are tender. Remove from the heat, place a clean tea towel over the pan and leave to sit for 10 minutes to allow the grains to fluff up.

Finely slice the rainbow chard leaves and stalks, keeping them separate. In a frying pan, heat 1 tablespoon of olive oil, add the chard stalks and sauté for 3–4 minutes over a medium heat until tender. Add the chard leaves and sauté for another 2 minutes until the leaves are wilted and the stalks are cooked through.

Combine the rainbow chard, bulgur wheat, roasted cauliflower and parsley. Spoon over the remaining tarator, drizzle over a little olive oil and squeeze over the lemon juice. Serve topped with the toasted almonds.

BASIL–LEMON SCENTED MILLET
WITH ROASTED BROCCOLI

Millet is an ancient grain with big health benefits – it is rich in iron, B vitamins and calcium and is a perfect naturally gluten-free alternative to couscous or barley. As a younger vegetarian, I often used millet to make burgers and bakes, but lately, I have rediscovered the delicious versatility of this grain in salads. It is fluffy, like rice or quinoa, but has a subtle corn taste and a lovely lightness which pairs wonderfully with herby oils. Here, millet is scented with a light and airy basil–lemon oil that reminds me of the warm evenings and cooling breezes of summer in Sydney.

GF | SERVES 4~6

2 broccoli heads (about 1 kg), cut into florets
2–3 tablespoons extra-virgin olive oil
1 litre (4 cups) vegetable stock or broth,
  plus extra if necessary
400 g millet
1 cup baby rocket leaves
½ cup basil leaves, torn
3 tablespoons roughly chopped flat-leaf
  parsley leaves
60 g parmesan, shaved
3 tablespoons sunflower seeds, toasted
sea salt and black pepper

BASIL–LEMON OIL

1 garlic clove, very finely chopped
1 cup basil leaves, torn
185 ml (¾ cup) extra-virgin olive oil
3 tablespoons grapeseed oil or other
  neutral oil
zest and juice of 1 lemon
sea salt and black pepper

SUBSTITUTES/OPTIONS

millet: couscous, pearl barley or quinoa
  (for gluten free)
For vegans, omit parmesan

Preheat the oven to 200°C.

In a large bowl, coat the broccoli in 1–2 tablespoons of olive oil and season with salt and pepper. Spread the broccoli on a baking tray and roast for 20–25 minutes, until golden and just tender.

To make the basil–lemon oil, put the garlic, basil and 1 tablespoon of water into the bowl of a food processor and blitz together until you have a green paste. Add the oils and lemon zest and blitz again, gradually squeezing in the lemon juice and tasting as you go to achieve a balanced, tangy oil. Season well with salt and pepper. Alternatively, pound the ingredients together using a mortar and pestle for a thicker end result.

Bring the vegetable stock to the boil in a large saucepan. Add the millet, cover with a lid and simmer over a low heat until all the stock has been absorbed and the grains are tender. (Add more stock or water if you need to, as some brands of millet take longer to cook than others.) Turn off the heat, remove the lid and leave the millet to sit for 10 minutes to allow the grains to dry out further and fluff up. Once cool, add the basil–lemon oil to the millet and mix well.

To serve, combine the broccoli with the millet, rocket and herbs and season with salt and pepper. Drizzle with olive oil and top with the shaved parmesan and sunflower seeds.

GREEN AND GOLD SALAD OF ASPARAGUS AND GOLD BEETROOT WITH FARRO, CRISPY SAGE AND LEMON BROWN BUTTER

While bursting with hues of green and gold, the colours of my native Australia, this dish emphatically embraces the seasonal produce of New York's farmers' markets. In late spring to early summer, it is with great anticipation that we welcome the abundant arrival of sunny gold beetroot and robust asparagus at local Greenmarkets and organic providores. To me, both ingredients absolutely encapsulate the flavour of trans-seasonal nature and earth. The lemon-scented brown butter dressing is something else, taking the classically pleasing combination of burnt butter and sage on a grand adventure.

SERVES 4~6

350 g farro, rinsed
1 garlic clove, crushed
4 large gold beetroot (about 1 kg),
    peeled and cut into thin wedges
3–4 tablespoons extra-virgin olive oil
400 g asparagus, trimmed and cut into
    2.5 cm pieces
1 cup microgreen sprouts (optional)
1 cup walnuts, toasted
sea salt and black pepper

LEMON BROWN BUTTER

120 g unsalted butter
½ cup sage leaves
juice of ½ lemon
1 small garlic clove, very finely chopped
¾ teaspoon dijon mustard
1 teaspoon maple syrup
sea salt

SUBSTITUTES

gold beetroot: red or target beetroot

Preheat the oven to 200°C.

Add the farro and crushed garlic to a saucepan of boiling salted water and cook for 20 minutes, or until tender. Drain.

Place the beetroot on a large baking tray, drizzle over 1–2 tablespoons of olive oil and season with salt. Roast for 25–30 minutes until tender.

Heat 1 tablespoon of olive oil in a large frying pan. Add the asparagus and cook for 1½–2 minutes until just tender but still bright green in colour.

To make the lemon brown butter, melt the butter in a small saucepan over a medium heat. Add the sage leaves and swirl around in the butter until they begin to crisp, then remove them from the pan, sprinkle over a little salt and leave to drain on absorbent paper towel. Continue to heat the butter until it is browned and smells nutty, then remove from the heat and leave to cool slightly. Carefully whisk in the lemon juice, garlic, mustard and maple syrup and add a pinch of salt.

Combine the farro, beetroot and asparagus, drizzle over a little olive oil and season well with salt and pepper. Arrange on a large serving dish and spoon over the lemon brown butter. To serve, scatter over the sprouts, if you like, and the crispy sage leaves and walnuts.

ROASTED SWEET POTATO WITH LEEKS AND MUSTARD CROUTONS

This salad is a twist on classic potato and leek soup – such an effortless, comforting combination. I've shaken up this classic just a little with the use of sweet potatoes and the addition of buttery mustard croutons and a creamy mustard dressing. And I'll let you in on a little tip – sometimes I do strange things in the kitchen, like blitz up leftover salads into soups (read about it on page 26)! I did just that with this salad (without the croutons) and I can attest that sweet potato and leek makes a rather nice soup too!

SERVES 4~6

6 sweet potatoes (about 1.4 kg), unpeeled, washed and cut into 1 cm cubes
4 small leeks, white and light green parts only, finely sliced into rounds and washed
2–3 tablespoons extra-virgin olive oil
3 tablespoons finely chopped chives
2 cups baby rocket leaves
sea salt and black pepper

MUSTARD CROUTONS

100 g salted butter
2 tablespoons dijon mustard
1 teaspoon thyme leaves
3 teaspoons finely chopped flat-leaf parsley leaves
250 g stale bread, such as sourdough or ciabatta, torn into 2 cm chunks
30 g parmesan, grated
sea salt and black pepper

MUSTARD DRESSING

250 g Greek yoghurt
1½ tablespoons dijon mustard
2 tablespoons extra-virgin olive oil
1 garlic clove, grated
sea salt and black pepper

Preheat the oven to 200°C.

For the mustard croutons, melt the butter in a saucepan over a medium heat until it starts to foam. Whisk in the mustard, herbs and a big pinch of salt and pepper, take off the heat and leave to cool for a few minutes. Spread the bread pieces out on a large baking tray, pour over the mustard butter and sprinkle over the grated cheese. Mix everything together well to ensure the bread is evenly coated. Bake for about 15 minutes or until the croutons are golden. Set aside to cool.

Arrange the sweet potato and leeks on a large baking tray. Drizzle over 1–2 tablespoons of olive oil and season with salt and pepper. Roast for 20–25 minutes until the vegetables are soft.

To make the mustard dressing, combine the yoghurt, mustard, oil and garlic. Whisk until smooth. Add a little water if it is too thick – you want the consistency of thickened cream. Season with salt and pepper to taste.

Combine the sweet potato and leeks with the chives, rocket and mustard croutons. To serve, stir through the dressing, drizzle with olive oil and season with salt and pepper.

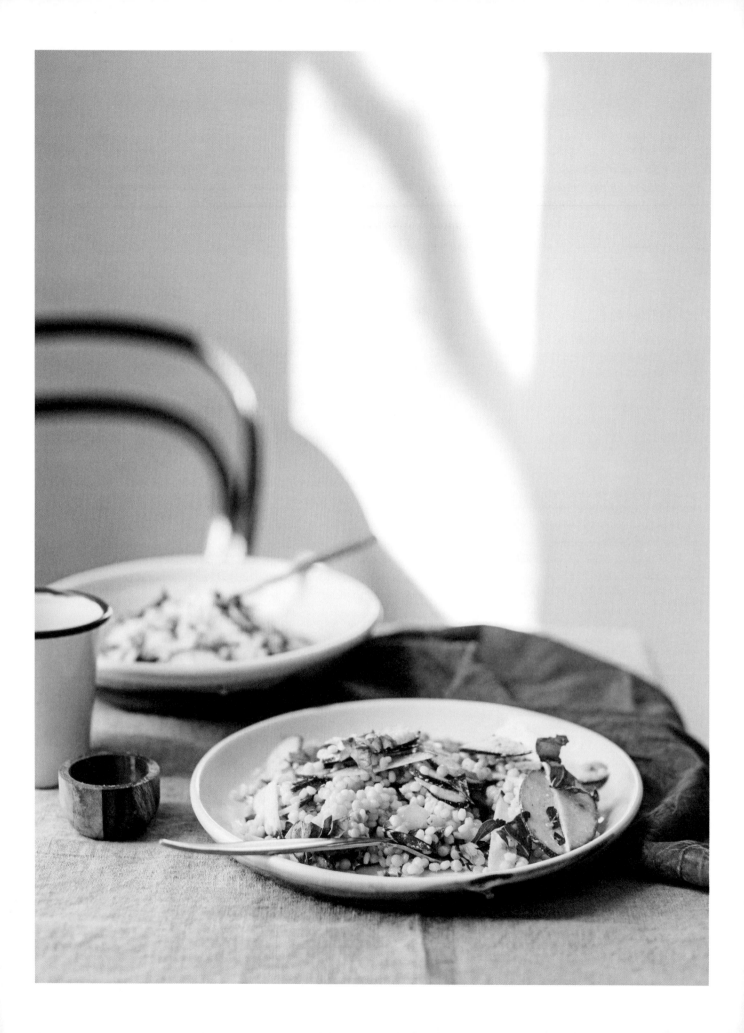

SHAVED ZUCCHINI WITH PEARL COUSCOUS AND CHILLI–LEMON RICOTTA

In the early days of Arthur Street Kitchen, I discovered the deliciousness of whipped up feta paired with zucchini. This salad is Part Two of that original recipe, a variation that sees creamy ricotta laced with chilli flakes and lemon zest, served with raw shaved zucchini and luscious balls of pearl couscous. Make room for this salad in your repertoire of family favourites!

SERVES 4~6

400 g pearl couscous
5 zucchini (about 700 g)
½ cup flat-leaf parsley leaves,
    roughly chopped
½ cup basil leaves, torn
1–2 tablespoons extra-virgin olive oil
3 tablespoons slivered almonds, toasted
sea salt and black pepper

CHILLI–LEMON RICOTTA

500 g ricotta
1 small garlic clove, very finely chopped
1–2 pinches of red chilli flakes
zest and juice of 1 lemon
2 tablespoons extra-virgin olive oil
125 g (½ cup) sour cream
sea salt and black pepper

Bring a large saucepan of salted water to the boil. Add the pearl couscous, stir well to prevent the balls from sticking and simmer for 6–8 minutes until the couscous is tender. Drain.

Using a mandoline, food processor or box grater, shave the zucchini into very thin slices.

To make the chilli–lemon ricotta, place the ricotta in a mixing bowl and add the garlic, chilli flakes, lemon zest and lemon juice. Whisk together. Add the olive oil, sour cream and 1–2 tablespoons of water to loosen up the cheese and give you the consistency of thickened cream. Season liberally with salt and pepper.

Combine the zucchini with the pearl couscous and herbs. Fold through the chilli–lemon ricotta, add a final swig of olive oil and season well with salt and pepper. To serve, scatter over the toasted almonds.

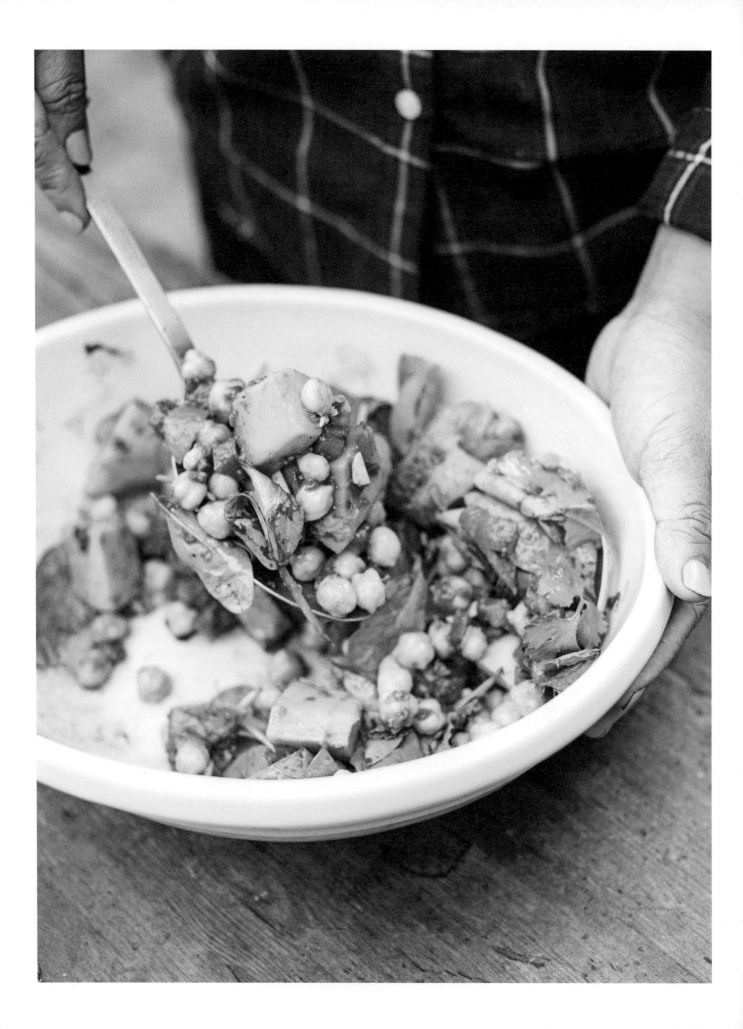

SPICED EGGPLANT AND TOMATO RELISH WITH ROASTED BUTTERNUT PUMPKIN AND CHICKPEAS

This spiced eggplant and tomato relish is my Christmas gifting staple. Packed into pretty jars, this is the most delicious edible gift, to be enjoyed over the holidays with cheese and crackers. When not gifting, pair this relish with sweet roasted butternut pumpkin and chickpeas for a hearty, vegetable-packed salad. This dish definitely exudes a fancy festive attitude.

VG | GF | SERVES 4~6

1 butternut pumpkin (about 1.4 kg),
    peeled and cut into 2 cm cubes
2 tablespoons extra-virgin olive oil
500 g cooked chickpeas
    (about 2 cans), drained
2 cups baby spinach leaves
1/2 cup mint leaves
1/2 cup coriander leaves
3 tablespoons slivered almonds, toasted
sea salt and black pepper

SPICED EGGPLANT AND TOMATO RELISH

80 ml (1/3 cup) extra-virgin olive oil
2 eggplants (about 800 g), peeled and
    cut into 1 cm cubes
1 onion, coarsely chopped
1 tablespoon yellow mustard seeds
2.5 cm piece of ginger, peeled and grated
1 long green chilli, deseeded and
    finely chopped
2 garlic cloves, finely chopped
1 tablespoon ground cumin
3 whole cloves
2 teaspoons paprika
1/2 teaspoon ground turmeric
400 g diced tomatoes (about 1 can)
3 tablespoons apple cider vinegar
115 g (1/2 cup) caster sugar
sea salt

SUBSTITUTES

butternut pumpkin: any variety of pumpkin,
    sweet potato, cauliflower
chickpeas: butterbeans, lentils

Preheat the oven to 200°C.

Place the butternut pumpkin on a large baking tray, drizzle with the olive oil and season with salt and pepper. Roast for 20–25 minutes until golden.

To make the relish, heat the oil in a large non-stick saucepan over a high heat. Add half the eggplant to the pan and cook for about 5 minutes, until tender and golden, then remove and set aside. Repeat with the remaining eggplant. Reduce the heat to medium, add the onion to the pan and cook, stirring often, for 3–4 minutes until soft, then add the mustard seeds and cook for about 2 minutes, until the seeds start to pop. Add the ginger, chilli, garlic, cumin, cloves, paprika, turmeric and a large pinch of salt and cook for a further 2 minutes. Return the eggplant to the pan along with the tomatoes, vinegar, sugar and 125 ml (1/2 cup) of water. Reduce the heat to low, cover with a lid and simmer, stirring occasionally, for 15–20 minutes until the mixture thickens and the eggplant is very soft.

Combine the pumpkin, chickpeas and baby spinach and spoon over the relish. Mix everything together well, then scatter over the herbs and slivered almonds to serve.

FRIED BUTTERBEANS AND PEARL BARLEY WITH BABY SPINACH AND CHILLI–HERB YOGHURT

This recipe goes to show how being well stocked with a few larder basics can produce a knockout salad! Canned legumes, spices, some dried grains, a few fridge greens and a tub of yoghurt can give you this super tasty dish. As always, substitute where needed – chickpeas also work well here, while you can use any grain or cereal you have on hand such as quinoa, freekeh or spelt.

SERVES 4~6

300 g pearl barley, rinsed
3–4 tablespoons extra-virgin olive oil
1 garlic clove, very finely chopped
1 teaspoon ground cumin
2 teaspoons ground coriander
1 teaspoon paprika
500 g cooked butterbeans
    (about 2 cans), drained
½ cup flat-leaf parsley leaves
    (or other soft herb), finely chopped
3 cups baby spinach leaves
juice of ½ lemon
sea salt and black pepper

CHILLI–HERB YOGHURT

1 long green or red chilli
500 g (2 cups) Greek yoghurt
1 small garlic clove, very finely chopped
1 tablespoon chopped mint, dill or
    parsley leaves
2 tablespoons extra-virgin olive oil
squeeze of lemon juice
sea salt and black pepper

Place the pearl barley in a large saucepan with plenty of salted water. Bring to the boil and simmer for 30–35 minutes until the barley is tender but retains a chewy bite. Drain.

Heat 1–2 tablespoons of olive oil in a large frying pan over a medium–high heat and add the garlic, cumin, coriander and paprika. Fry for 30 seconds until the spices are fragrant, then add the drained butterbeans and season with a generous amount of salt and pepper. Stir to coat the beans in the spices and fry until the beans are crisp and golden, shaking the pan every now and then to move the beans around and adding more olive oil as needed. Set aside.

To make the chilli–herb yoghurt, halve the chilli, reserving the seeds for later, and finely chop the flesh. Combine the yoghurt with the garlic, chilli, herbs, olive oil and lemon juice. Season with salt and pepper to taste. If you would like the yoghurt hotter, add some of the reserved chilli seeds.

Combine the pearl barley with the parsley, baby spinach and fried butterbeans and drizzle with olive oil. Season with salt and pepper and mix well. To serve, spread the chilli–herb yoghurt across a large serving platter. Spoon the bean and barley mixture on top of the yoghurt and squeeze over the lemon juice to finish.

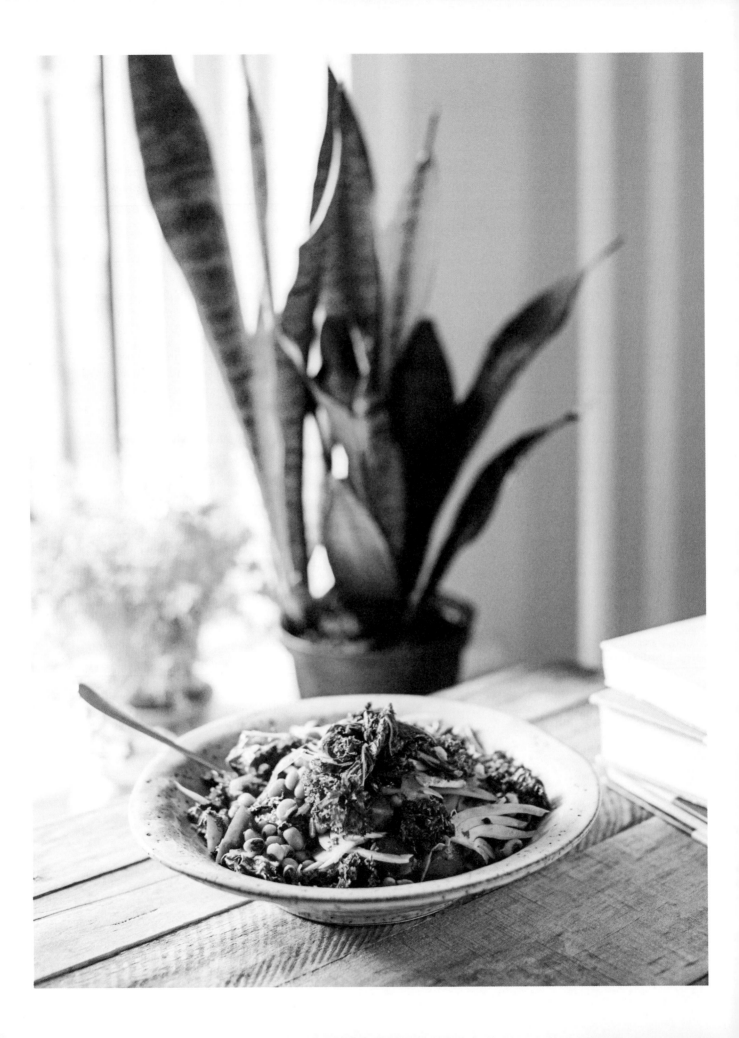

BLACK EYE BEANS WITH KALE, FENNEL, CHERRY TOMATOES AND FENNEL SEED OIL

As a kid, I was fascinated by my mother's secret pantry, full of the exotic ingredients she used in her medicinal broths. Amongst the ginseng and mystery jars of horns, antlers and bones, there always sat a bottle of black eye beans. So for me, this salad definitely packs a medicinal punch – a simple dish of wholesome black eye beans, teamed with nutrient-rich kale, fennel, tomatoes and a surprising fennel seed oil.

VG | GF | SERVES 4~6

400 g dried black eye beans, rinsed
2 garlic cloves, crushed with a heavy knife
1 tablespoon olive oil
½ bunch of kale leaves, washed thoroughly, central stems removed, leaves torn
2 fennel bulbs (about 800 g)
200 g cherry tomatoes
½ cup basil leaves
3 tablespoons sunflower seeds, toasted
sea salt and black pepper

FENNEL SEED OIL

1 tablespoon fennel seeds
1 garlic clove
½ cup basil leaves
1 teaspoon sea salt
120 ml extra-virgin olive oil
zest of ½ lemon
black pepper

SUBSTITUTES

dried black eye beans: canned black eye beans
cherry tomatoes: any other tomato variety, diced

Place the black eye beans in a saucepan with one of the garlic cloves, cover with water and bring to the boil. Add a large pinch of salt, reduce the heat to medium and simmer, covered, for 30–35 minutes until the beans are tender but still holding their shape. Drain and leave to cool, then break up the garlic with the back of a fork and stir through the beans.

For the fennel seed oil, add the fennel seeds to a small frying pan over a medium heat and toast for 60 seconds, or until the seeds start to pop and smell aromatic. Tip the toasted seeds into a mortar and pound with a pestle, then add the garlic, basil and salt and pound to a rough paste. Stir in the olive oil and lemon zest and season with pepper.

Heat the olive oil in a frying pan, add the kale, remaining crushed garlic and a pinch of salt and cook over a medium heat for 2–3 minutes until the kale is wilted.

Finely slice the fennel with a mandoline, food processor or sharp knife. Roughly chop the tomatoes.

Combine the black eye beans with the kale, fennel, tomatoes and basil. Pour the fennel seed oil over and toss together. For maximum flavour, let this salad sit and marinate for 30 minutes to enable the flavours to come together. When ready to eat, scatter over the sunflower seeds.

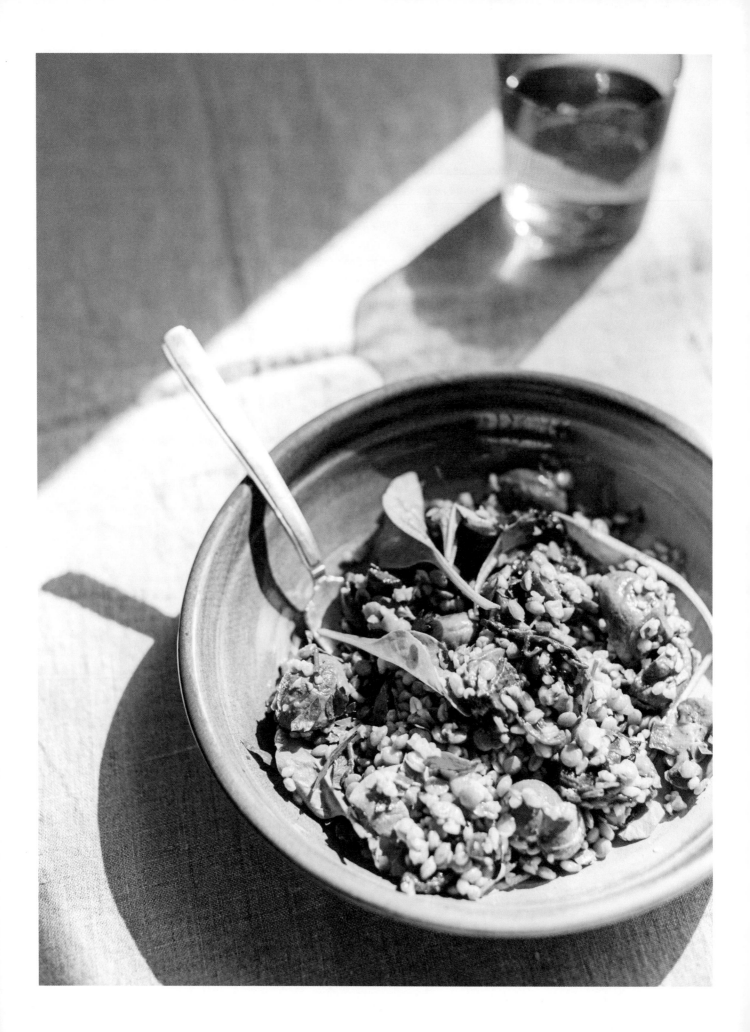

BEER-MARINATED MUSHROOMS WITH GREEN LENTILS AND FREEKEH

My former neighbourhood of Surry Hills was a creative hub. On Arthur Street where I lived and worked, we were ethical fashion designers, candle-makers, rug-makers, salad-makers, craft beer brewers and more. Our street corners were our meeting rooms, where we would laugh, chat and brainstorm. This salad was conceived around the corner on Bourke Street, when I ran into my neighbour Matt King, one third of local brewer The Grifter Brewing Co. The Grifter make rich, full-flavoured hand-crafted ales and I wondered how one of their beers would taste in a salad. So this wacky little marriage of beer and mushrooms was born. Use whichever ale you like, making sure it's full bodied and delicious.

SERVES 4~6

30 g dried porcini mushrooms
750 g button mushrooms, cleaned
200 g green lentils, rinsed
200 g freekeh, rinsed
1–2 tablespoons extra-virgin olive oil
1 garlic clove, finely chopped
2 teaspoons finely chopped rosemary leaves
20 g salted butter
1 cup baby spinach leaves
3 tablespoons roughly chopped
   flat-leaf parsley leaves
3 tablespoons finely sliced chives
juice of ½ lemon
150 g fresh ricotta, crumbled
sea salt and black pepper

BEER MARINADE

700 ml ale
150 ml orange juice
2.5 cm piece of ginger, peeled and
   finely chopped
1 long red chilli, deseeded and
   finely chopped
2 eschalots (see note page 32), finely sliced
2 tablespoons honey
80 ml (⅓ cup) extra-virgin olive oil
2 teaspoons sea salt

SUBSTITUTES

button mushrooms: any variety
   of mushrooms

Place the porcini mushrooms in a bowl, cover with hot water and leave to soak for 10 minutes. Remove the porcini mushrooms from the soaking liquid, squeeze out any excess liquid with your hands and set aside. Reserve a few tablespoons of the mushroom soaking liquid, being sure to avoid the grit at the bottom of the bowl, and discard the rest.

For the beer marinade, combine all the ingredients in a large bowl together with the reserved mushroom soaking liquid and mix well. Add the button and porcini mushrooms to the marinade and leave to marinate in the refrigerator for at least 1 hour, preferably overnight.

Add the lentils and freekeh to a saucepan of salted water. Bring to the boil and cook for 20–25 minutes until both are just tender. Drain and set aside.

Heat 1 tablespoon of olive oil in a large frying pan, throw in the garlic and rosemary, then add the mushrooms and a few tablespoons of the marinade and fry until the mushrooms are golden (you may have to do this in batches). Remove from the heat and add the butter.

Combine the mushrooms, lentils, freekeh, spinach, parsley and chives. Drizzle over some olive oil, squeeze over the lemon and spoon over a little more of the beer marinade. To serve, scatter over the ricotta and season with salt and pepper.

HOMEMADE PANEER WITH LIME-PICKLED CAULIFLOWER AND BLACK EYE BEANS

The wonderful thing about neighbourhoods is the wealth of knowledge gained from transient sidewalk chats, at school drop off, or at the local park. This recipe is rooted in a cauliflower salad recipe from my Surry Hills neighbourhood friend Gayu Mudaliar. Her clever and simple Indian-style dish was the inspiration for this whole-hearted salad, complete with homemade paneer and lashings of lime juice. Paneer is really easy to make – all you need is milk and lemon juice. Eat this creamy, mild cheese straight away. And since it doesn't melt, it is robust enough to use in curries and salads, like I have here.

GF | SERVES 4~6

1 cauliflower head (about 750 g),
   cut into small florets
juice of 4 limes
3–4 tablespoons extra-virgin olive oil
2 teaspoons cumin seeds
1 small garlic clove, very finely chopped
500 g cooked black eye beans
   (about 2 cans), drained
1 long green chilli, deseeded and
   finely chopped
2 cm piece of ginger, peeled and
   finely chopped
3 tablespoons black sesame seeds
3 tablespoons white sesame seeds, toasted
2 tablespoons nigella seeds
½ cup coriander leaves
sea salt and black pepper

PANEER

4 litres full-cream milk
120 ml lemon juice, plus extra if necessary

SUBSTITUTES

homemade paneer: store-bought paneer
black eye beans: chickpeas

Place the cauliflower florets in a ceramic bowl (or other non-reactive bowl) and add half the lime juice and 2 teaspoons of salt. Cover and leave to pickle for at least 2 hours, but the longer the better. You can even leave it to pickle overnight in the refrigerator.

Line a colander with a clean muslin cloth or thin cotton material. To make the paneer, heat the milk in a large saucepan and bring to a slow boil. When the milk starts to rise, stir in the lemon juice. Keep stirring until the milk splits (add more lemon juice if you need to) – eventually, the solid curds will separate from the watery whey. Remove from the heat and pour into the muslin-lined colander to drain off the whey. Press the curd together to form the paneer, rinse in cold water and fold up the sides of the muslin to form a little bundle. Leave in the colander, put a weight over the top (like a bowl filled with water) and leave it to drain for about 15 minutes.

In a small frying pan, add 2 tablespoons of olive oil and when hot, fry the cumin seeds and garlic for a minute or so, until fragrant. Immediately pour over the cauliflower and mix well.

Crumble up the paneer with your fingers and scatter over the cauliflower. Add the black eye beans, remaining lime juice, a drizzle of olive oil, green chilli, ginger and a big pinch of salt. Mix well. To serve, scatter over the black and white sesame seeds, nigella seeds and coriander leaves.

CHARGRILLED BROCCOLI RABE AND WITLOF WITH COS LETTUCE, WALNUTS AND STILTON CREAM

One of the truly wonderful things about food is its innate ability to invoke memories and taste-induced nostalgia. When I eat broccoli and Stilton soup, I am instantly transported to a little thatched-roof English pub in the countryside. This salad is a homage to this memory but is somehow less English alehouse and more modern Australian beer garden. It pairs broccoli rabe, or rapini as it is commonly known in some parts of the world, with a creamy, smooth yet punchy Stilton cream. This salad is one of contrasts, with the slight bitterness of the broccoli rabe, witlof and walnuts beautifully tempered by the creamy dressing.

GF | SERVES 4~6

1 kg broccoli rabe, trimmed and
cut into 5 cm pieces
2 witlof (about 220 g), trimmed and
cut into thin wedges
1–2 tablespoons extra-virgin olive oil
1 cos lettuce (about 500 g), halved
lengthways and roughly sliced into
thick segments
3 tablespoons finely chopped chives
1 cup walnuts, toasted and crushed
sea salt and black pepper

STILTON CREAM

1 tablespoon extra-virgin olive oil
1 garlic clove
125 g (½ cup) crème fraîche or
light sour cream
200 g Stilton, crumbled
pinch of ground nutmeg
1 tablespoon finely chopped chives
black pepper

SUBSTITUTES

broccoli rabe: broccoli, broccolini
Stilton: another creamy, soft blue cheese
like Gorgonzola

Preheat a griddle pan or barbecue to high.

Lightly coat the broccoli rabe and witlof with the olive oil and season with salt. Place the broccoli rabe on the pan or barbecue and cook until slightly charred on each side. Continue until all the broccoli rabe is cooked. Then add the witlof wedges and cook for only 30 seconds per side, just enough to soften and get some char marks on the leaves. You don't want them wilted.

To make the Stilton cream, add the olive oil and garlic to a small saucepan and cook for 10 seconds. Pour in the crème fraîche and heat on low heat. Add the Stilton and stir to melt the cheese. Stir in the nutmeg and chives and finish with lots of pepper.

Arrange the cos lettuce on a large plate or serving board. Place the broccoli rabe and witlof on top and sprinkle over the chives and toasted walnuts. Spoon over the Stilton cream and season lightly with pepper.

JUST BRING DESSERT

Like salads, there is something deeply social and inclusive about desserts. Embracing this collaborative spirit, this chapter is written with a little help from my friends. The sweet-makers in this chapter hail from three different continents and have generously shared their ultimate 'just bring dessert' recipes that they love to make and take to a social gathering.

These show-stopping yet simple recipes are delivered to us with an honest passion, against the backdrop of charming stories and memories of food, family and friendship.

Hetty McKinnon

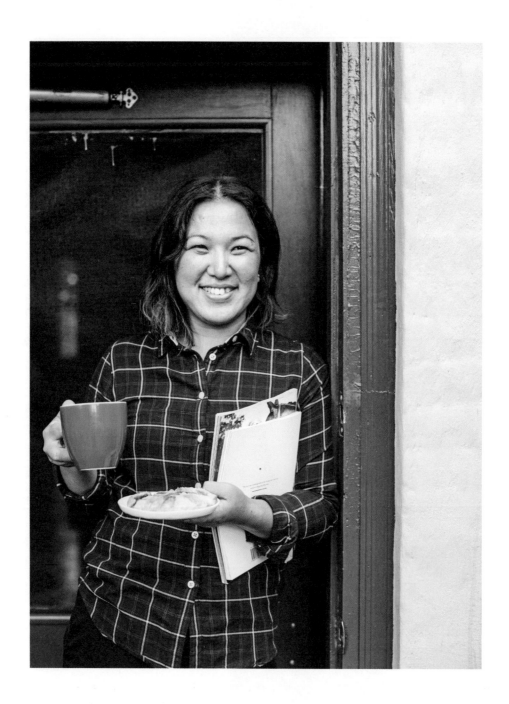

CARROLL GARDENS, BROOKLYN (USA)

Hetty will be bringing

SALTED CARAMEL AND APPLE GALETTES

As many of you may know, my career in food started with baking French macarons for a local cafe (owned by my dear friends Remy and Lee) in Surry Hills, Sydney. In those days, I relentlessly chased perfection in my baking. Batches upon batches of imperfect macarons were discarded. I soon learned that making macarons in a non-temperature controlled home kitchen, amidst the humidity of Sydney was not exactly ideal. That career was never going to last.

Still, my short-lived macaron-making business taught me a lot about flavour combinations. It was while making macarons that I discovered the wonders of salt and caramel. My love of this flavour combination led me to this new classic, an incredibly indulgent dessert of fresh seasonal apples laced in salted caramel, wrapped in an incredibly crumbly pie pastry.

These galettes are made in three parts. First, there is the shortcrust, which I have brazenly coined the 'best-ever'. I am willing to go out on a limb here and back my claim 100 per cent. I have made this crust many times and on every occasion it has turned out flaky, melty and delicious. The best thing of all, you don't need any apparatus to make it, just your fingertips! Next, there is the filling, which is simply apple and spices. The last (but not least) component is the salted caramel – this caramel recipe is super easy and fairly fail-proof, but you do have to exercise caution when you add in the butter and cream as it bubbles quite violently!

SALTED CARAMEL AND APPLE GALETTES

This quantity of pastry is enough to make a traditional 22 cm double crust apple pie. If making a pie, just halve the pastry before you chill it – roll out one half for the bottom of the pie, then use the other half for the pie top. For these galettes, I used golden delicious apples, but use whichever apples you have on hand, or even two different varieties. If you have any salted caramel remaining after making the galettes, you can store this in an airtight container in the fridge for 2 weeks (just warm it up before you use it!).

MAKES 6 INDIVIDUAL GALETTES

BEST-EVER SHORTCRUST PASTRY

300 g (2 cups) plain flour, plus extra
    for rolling
3 tablespoons caster sugar
1 teaspoon salt
175 g cold unsalted butter
125 ml (½ cup) cold full-cream milk,
    plus extra for glazing

FILLING

2–3 apples (about 400 g), peeled
juice of 1 lemon
2 tablespoons soft brown sugar
¾ teaspoon ground cinnamon
small pinch of ground nutmeg
½ teaspoon vanilla extract

SALTED CARAMEL

115 g (½ cup) caster sugar
50 g salted butter
3 tablespoons pouring cream
2 teaspoons sea salt, plus extra
    for sprinkling

To make the pastry, add the flour, sugar, salt and cold butter to a large bowl. Using your fingertips, work the butter into the flour, until you get pea-sized pieces. You don't need to work it too much at this point. If you still see little blobs of butter, that is fine – it will all add to the melt-in-your-mouth quality of the pastry. Add the cold milk and mix until a dough forms. Do not over mix. The less you work the dough at this point, the flakier (or to use the pastry term, short) your dough will be. Wrap the dough in plastic wrap and leave to rest for at least 1 hour in the refrigerator (or even overnight!).

Note: Keeping your pastry as cold as possible means that the fat won't melt before baking. When the lumps of fat melt in the oven as the pastry bakes, it results in lots of flaky layers and extra deliciousness!

For the filling, if you have an apple corer, core the apples. Using a mandoline or very sharp knife, finely slice the apples all the way through the centre so you get nice round slices. If you don't have an apple corer, slice the apples first, then use a sharp paring knife to dig out the cores. Place the apple slices in a bowl and squeeze over the lemon juice to prevent browning and to add flavour. Next, add the brown sugar, cinnamon, nutmeg and vanilla.

To make the salted caramel, heat the sugar in a saucepan with 2 tablespoons of water. Stir constantly for 4–5 minutes with a wooden spoon or heat resistant rubber spatula. The sugar will eventually melt and turn into an amber coloured liquid. At this point, very carefully add the butter to the sugar mixture and stir until melted. The mixture will bubble as the butter melts. Finally, slowly pour in the cream, taking great care as the hot mixture will rise in the pan and bubble quite rapidly at this point. Once combined, remove from the heat and add the sea salt.

Preheat the oven to 180°C. Line a baking tray with baking paper.

Flour your surface and roll out your cold pastry until it is about 3 mm thick. Using a plate or bowl, carefully cut out 6 rounds – my pastry rounds measured 16 cm each. Transfer the pastry rounds onto the lined baking tray and spread about 2 teaspoons of salted caramel in the middle

of each round, leaving a 2.5 cm border around the outside. Sprinkle a few sea salt flakes over the caramel. Pile the apples on top of the caramel, then fold the pastry edges over the apples, pleating to hold the fruit in. Add an extra dollop of salted caramel to the exposed fruit. Brush the pastry with milk and bake in the oven for 30–35 minutes, until it is golden.

Best eaten with vanilla ice cream!

Hetty will also be bringing

SLICE, THREE WAYS

I adore the simplicity and charm of an old-fashioned country slice. To me, it is a very Australian dessert, reminiscent of traditional school fetes or country fairs. Super simple to make, thrown together with pantry ingredients, a slice is my perfect accompaniment to a cup of tea.

I have been making slices to go with salads since the very beginning of Arthur Street Kitchen. A slice is a perfect vice to a salad's virtue. Over the years, I have developed a number of tasty slices that are essentially variations of the one basic recipe.

Each slice starts with a biscuit base, layered with a sweet filling of either caramel, curd or fruit and topped with either chocolate or toasted coconut. If you are looking for a knockout, absolute beginner, fail-safe sweet recipe, this is it!

FIRST WAY | *LEMON CURD AND COCONUT SLICE*

MAKES ABOUT 20 SQUARES

SLICE BASE

90 g (1 cup) desiccated coconut
230 g (1 cup) soft brown sugar
150 g (1 cup) self-raising flour
125 g salted butter, melted

**LEMON CURD
(MAKES ABOUT 375 G/1 CUP)**

3 large eggs
80 ml (⅓ cup) lemon juice, strained
170 g (¾ cup) caster sugar
50 g unsalted butter, cut into small cubes
zest of 1 lemon (optional)

TOASTED COCONUT TOPPING

180 g (2 cups) desiccated or shredded coconut
115 g (½ cup) caster sugar
1 egg, beaten

Preheat the oven to 180°C. Grease and line a 25 x 30 cm lamington tray or slice tin with baking paper.

To make the base, combine the coconut, brown sugar, self-raising flour and melted butter. Press the mixture into the lined tray using the back of a wooden spoon to smooth out the surface. Bake for 8–10 minutes or until the base is a nice golden brown. Leave to cool.

For the lemon curd, put the eggs, lemon juice and sugar in a stainless steel bowl and mix well. Place this over a saucepan of simmering water and stir constantly until the mixture becomes the consistency of sour cream or hollandaise sauce (this will take about 10 minutes). Take off the heat and strain immediately. While still hot, whisk in the butter and lemon zest (if you are using).

Finally, for the coconut topping, combine the coconut, caster sugar and egg and mix until well combined.

Spread the lemon curd evenly over the base, smoothing it out with the back of a spoon. Scatter the coconut topping evenly over the curd and bake for 5–6 minutes until golden brown. When completely cool, cut into squares. These slices will keep in the fridge for up to 7 days.

SECOND WAY | *GRILLED BANANA AND COCONUT SLICE*

MAKES ABOUT 20 SQUARES

1 x quantity Slice Base (see above)
1 x quantity Toasted Coconut Topping
  (see above)

FILLING

3–4 bananas, sliced lengthways into 3 pieces
1 tablespoon soft brown sugar
395 g (about 1 can) sweetened
  condensed milk
3 tablespoons golden syrup
30 g salted butter

Preheat the oven to 180°C. Grease and line a 25 x 30 cm lamington tray or slice tin with baking paper.

Begin by caramelising the bananas. Heat your grill to a hot setting. Put the banana slices on a baking tray lined with baking paper and sprinkle over the brown sugar. Place under the hot grill and cook for 3–4 minutes, until the sugar on top starts to caramelise and turn golden. Leave to cool.

Press the slice base mixture into the lined tray, using the back of a wooden spoon to smooth out the surface. Bake for 8–10 minutes, or until the base is a nice golden brown. Leave to cool.

Combine the condensed milk, golden syrup and butter in a small, heavy-based saucepan and heat gently over a medium heat. Stir constantly until the butter melts and the mixture boils (you need to keep stirring, otherwise the mixture will burn on the bottom). Pour onto the base, arrange the caramelised bananas on top and return to the oven for another 8–10 minutes or until golden.

Spread the coconut topping evenly over the filling and bake for a further 5–6 minutes until golden brown. When completely cool, cut into squares. Slices can be stored in the fridge for up to 7 days.

THIRD WAY | *SALTED CARAMEL SLICE*

MAKES ABOUT 20 SQUARES

1 x quantity Slice Base (see opposite)

FILLING

395 g (about 1 can) sweetened
   condensed milk
80 ml (⅓ cup) golden syrup
50 g salted butter
2–3 teaspoons sea salt (vary according
   to how salty you like it)

TOPPING

200 g dark chocolate, broken into pieces

Preheat the oven to 180°C. Grease and line a 25 x 30 cm lamington tray or slice tin with baking paper.

Press the slice base mixture into the lined tray, using the back of a wooden spoon to smooth out the surface. Bake for 8–10 minutes, or until the base is a nice golden brown. Leave to cool.

For the filling, combine the condensed milk, golden syrup and butter in a small, heavy-based saucepan and heat gently over a medium heat. Stir constantly until the butter melts and the mixture comes to a simmer (you need to keep stirring, otherwise the mixture will burn on the bottom). Add your desired amount of salt. Pour onto the base and return to the oven for another 10 minutes or until the caramel is golden and bubbly. Set aside to cool.

To melt the chocolate, place it in a glass or stainless steel bowl. In a saucepan, bring some water to the boil – once boiling, turn off the heat. Immediately put the bowl of chocolate on top of the saucepan and leave it to melt – it should take 8–10 minutes. Once melted (it becomes glossy), stir until smooth.

Pour the melted dark chocolate over the caramel filling, smoothing with a flat spatula.

Once the chocolate has set, you are ready to cut into squares. To make cutting easier, I usually sit a knife in boiling water to heat it up. Once nice and hot, dry it off with a paper towel and cut your slices – having a heated knife will help stop the chocolate from cracking. These slices store in the fridge for at least 7 days.

Jennifer Wong

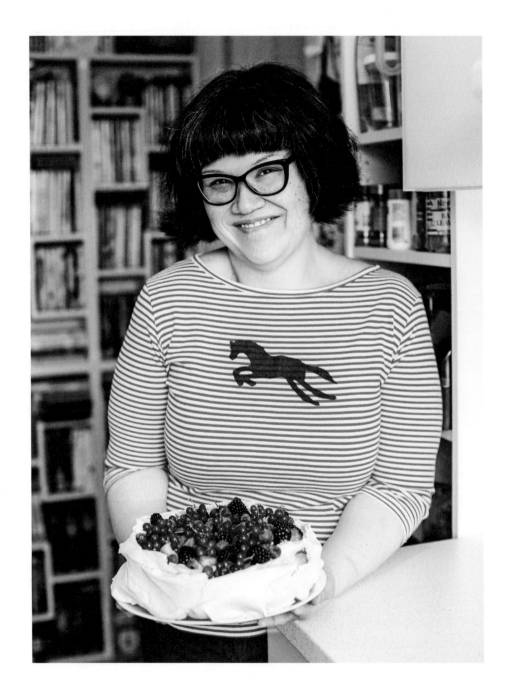

SURRY HILLS, SYDNEY (AUSTRALIA)

Jennifer will be bringing

CLASSIC PAVLOVA

Jen is one of my oldest friends. We met at university, where we bonded over movie marathons between lectures and seminars. While we both studied the social sciences and media, such are the mysteries of life that somehow I ended up tossing salads and Jen ended up as a really amazing lawyer.

Apart from our mutual love of cinema and, in particular, movies based on young adult fiction, we also share a love of food. Jen and I have attended countless cooking classes together, making everything from mozzarella and pastries to marshmallows, praline and brioche. There was also one shamefully failed attempt at making nougat, which we don't really talk about anymore (note, I have since rectified said disaster, to the chagrin of my overworked Kitchenaid mixer). I have known Jen to stay up into the wee hours, baking like there is no tomorrow. For every salad I have made, Jen has dished out a killer cake. She really is the sweet to my savoury. And while she makes a mean coconut cake and a terrific tiramisu, she is totally the queen of the pavlova, one of my favourite desserts.

For Jen, making pavlova is a labour of love – her recipe was her mother's, which she has now made her own.

'I am known for my pavlova. It is a New Year's favourite with my friends and highly sought after amongst my co-workers. My original pavlova recipe is contained in my old leather Filofax, quickly jotted down several years ago when talking to my mum on the telephone. I have modified my mum's recipe, experimenting with several versions. A good pav has a crisp outer shell and a creamy solid meringue filling that, when cut, can hold itself like a slice of cake, even with the weight of the fruit and cream on top. I include cream of tartar, cornflour and arrowroot to achieve this, however these ingredients are optional – without them I find that the pavlova is flatter and the meringue centre is less firm, but still delicious.'

CLASSIC PAVLOVA

My philosophy in regard to pavlova toppings is 'never say never'. My go-to topping is a layer of thickened cream covered with diced berries (whatever is in season) tossed through passionfruit pulp. In summer I love a layer of mascarpone and a layer of sliced mangoes, topped with toasted coconut.

SERVES 8

6 eggwhites
½ teaspoon cream of tartar (optional)
460 g (2 cups) caster sugar
1 teaspoon vanilla essence (or be
    adventurous and substitute with
    rosewater or orange blossom)
2 teaspoons white vinegar
1 tablespoon cornflour (optional)
2 tablespoons arrowroot (optional)

TO SERVE

200 ml thickened or whipped cream
seasonal fruit tossed with passionfruit pulp
    or raspberry coulis

Preheat the oven to 200°C. Line a baking tray with baking paper.

In a clean, dry bowl beat the eggwhites with an electric mixer on a medium–high speed until stiff peaks form. With the mixer still going, add the cream of tartar, if using, and slowly add the caster sugar a spoon at a time. You need to keep mixing until all the sugar dissolves and the meringue is glossy (I find this takes around 10 minutes).

Reduce the mixer speed to low and fold in the vanilla, white vinegar and the cornflour and arrowroot, if using.

Pile the meringue in the middle of the lined baking tray and using a knife (I use my grandmother's old butter knife) make a circle shape with a flat top and smooth sides (like you would ice a cake). The circumference should be the size of a dinner plate. Note: this is where I differ from my mum, she prefers to heap the pav into a rough circle on the baking tray with a slight well in the centre.

Place the meringue on the bottom shelf of your oven, shut the door and turn the oven down to 140–150°C. Cook for 70 minutes. The meringue should bake to a warm cream colour – if it's starting to look toasty in colour, turn the oven temperature down by 10°C. At no time during the baking should you open the oven door.

Turn the oven off and leave it to cool completely. To serve, layer with cream and fruit.

Essential pavlova tips from Jennifer:

The staler the eggwhite, the better the meringue.

Humidity is meringue's enemy. In humid conditions, your pavlova will be flat.

Bake it just before you go to bed. The best results come from never opening the oven door. I bake the pav for 1 hour 10 minutes, turn the oven off and leave it overnight. At a minimum, don't open the oven door until the oven has cooled completely.

Don't stress if your pavlova cracks, I don't understand people's obsession with avoiding cracks. The best thing about a pavlova is that you cover it with so much cream and fruit, no one cares about a perfect looking shell.

Wesley Verhoeve

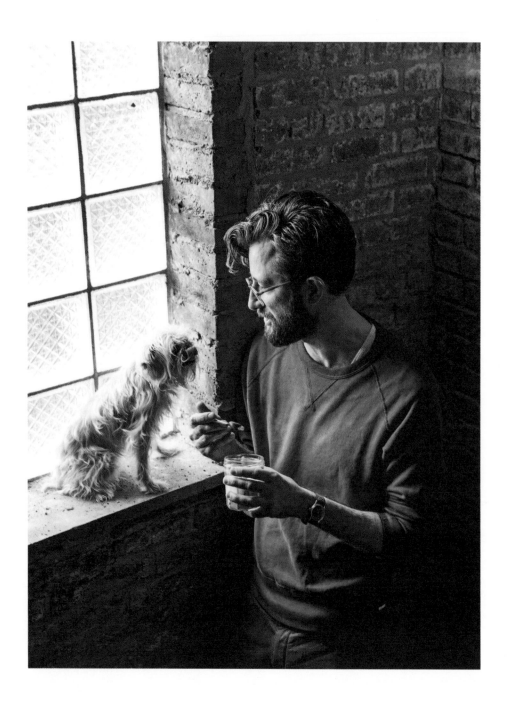

CLINTON HILL, BROOKLYN (USA)

Wesley will be bringing

RASPBERRY MOUSSE

Wesley is a modern man. He is a Brooklyn-based photographer, writer, documentarian and multi-disciplinary creative. Through his extraordinary photography project, One of Many, Wesley travels around the United States, camera in hand, exploring the creative communities of 12 American cities. Since my arrival in his home borough, he has been a great provider of tea and conversation.

Wesley, like myself, confesses to being 'not a dessert person'. He does, however, have one powerful sweet recipe up his sleeve. I have made this dessert several times already and I can assure you, it is a crowd pleaser. It is also the dessert that my children actually ask for, time and time again.

This raspberry mousse is Wesley's dinner party go-to:

'What I like best about this mousse is that it's visually appealing and it 'feels' impressive for guests, even though it's easy and requires few ingredients. I like making it in front of people, because you only want to prepare it mere minutes before people eat it. Making it is a little bit of a show and then you get the pay-off of watching people eat it right after. The recipe is something my grandmother used to make, as I'm sure many other grandmothers did in their day. To me it feels like a modern classic and I've passed it on to many friends because it's so great for dinner parties and making in volume.'

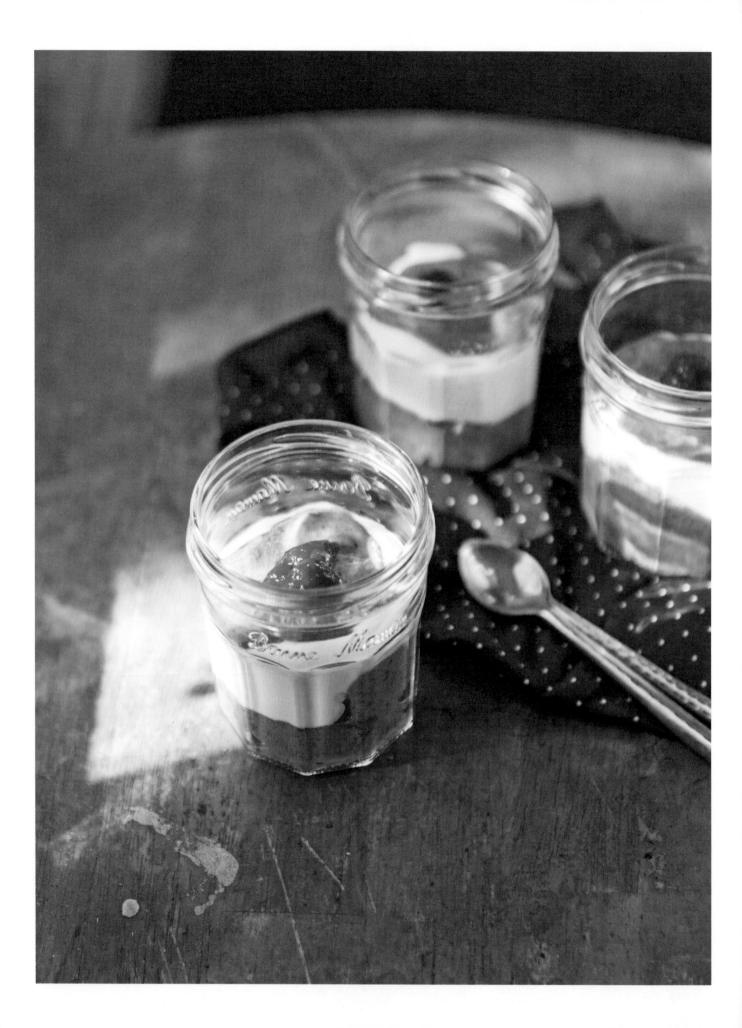

RASPBERRY MOUSSE

*Substitute the raspberries with other frozen fruit such as mixed berries,
blackberries or even mangoes.*

GF | SERVES 4

300 g frozen raspberries
2–3 tablespoons honey
5 eggwhites

TO SERVE (OPTIONAL)
fresh raspberries
whipped cream

Place the frozen raspberries in a small food processor or use
a hand-held blender and pulse to chop them up, keeping the
pieces quite large – you are looking for a rough puree.

Add the honey and pulse a bit more, then add the eggwhites
and process until it's all fluffy and smooth. The colour will have
lightened and the volume will have grown. This should only take
2 minutes.

Spoon a big dollop of the mousse into four glasses (like whiskey
glasses) and serve immediately, topping each with a puff of
whipped cream and some fresh berries, if you like.

Bianca Presto

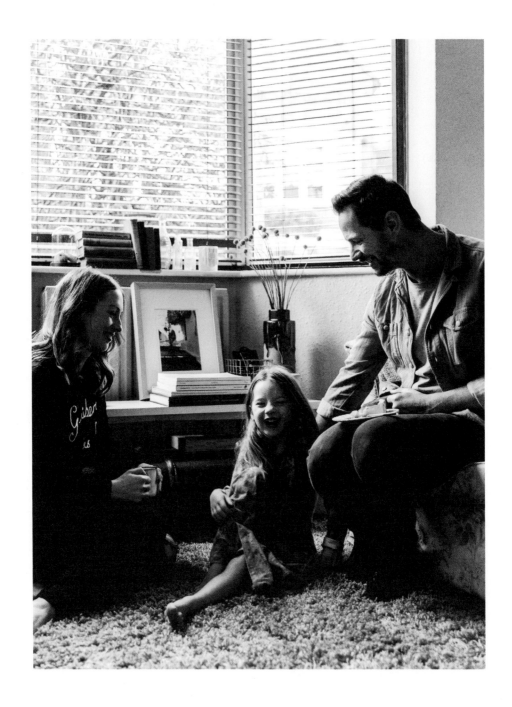

RADLETT, HERTFORDSHIRE (UK)

Bianca will be bringing

SOUTH AFRICAN MELKTERT (MILK TART)

I met Bianca over a decade ago in London, a day or so after the London bombings of 2005. I was interviewing her for a job. When Bianca turned up for our meeting, she was a little (or a lot) frazzled as she had just lost her mobile phone in the back of a black cab, adding to the sense of panic already pervasive in the air. From that first anxious meeting, I adored her complete lack of pretence and, of course, gave her the job. While we have lived in different cities for most of our friendship, somehow her South African feistiness and my Aussie sarcasm have made us long-time, long-distance mates who bond over a love of homemade bagels and baking adventures.

Bianca grew up in a family of feeders. And eaters, for that matter. During her childhood, Bianca's father ran a restaurant and in later years produced traditional boiled bagels based on a recipe from his great-grandmother.

Bianca remembers, 'My first job at 14 was working as a waitress in a Jewish delicatessen that my father managed at the time. My mother was the family's resident baker; no matter what the occasion, she always had an appropriate cake up her sleeve and my 14-year-old self still credits her with my "Best in Class" Home Economics award after she coached me to greatness with some perfectly formed spinach and gruyere vol-au-vents.

'My early memories of dating my now-husband Steve are steeped in food-related nostalgia. From the first meal I cooked for him in the hostel where we met (grilled chicken pieces dusted with crushed salt and vinegar crisps, an idea from my Granny Sheila) to the very first time I made him his absolute favourite dessert, a milk tart. To give it its proper name, "melktert" is a traditional South African dessert consisting of sweet pastry crust filled with a creamy cinnamon-infused custard. This recipe was given to mc by my mother, it was passed down to her by her grandmother and I think it may have just made my husband finally commit!'

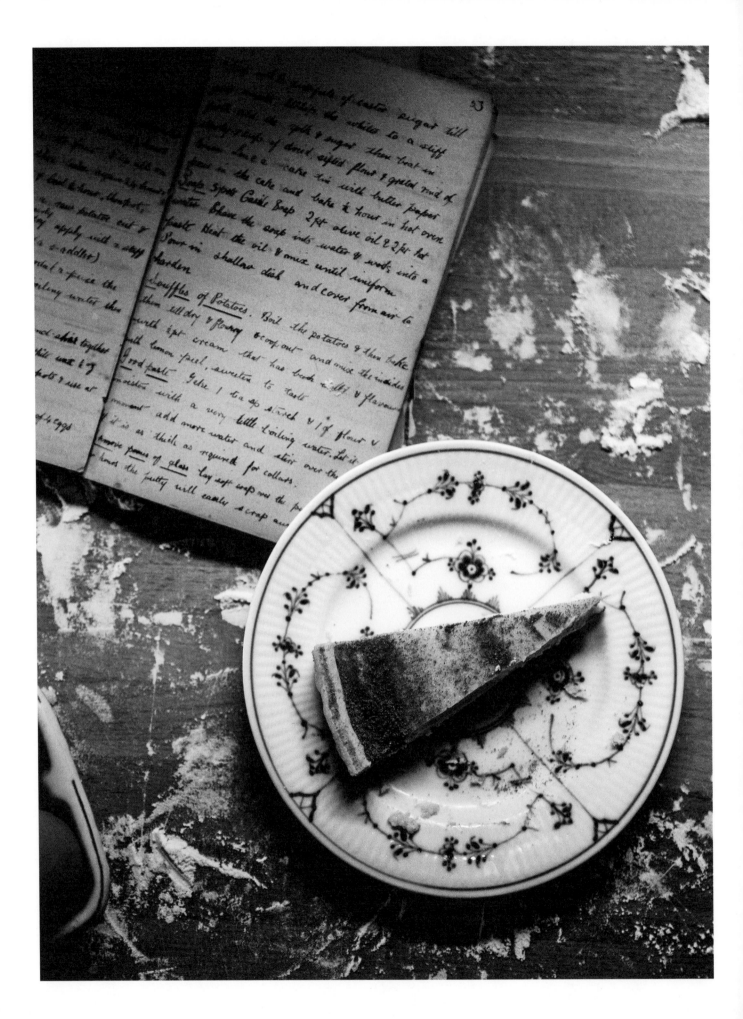

SOUTH AFRICAN MELKTERT (MILK TART)

For ease, or when we're baking with our daughter, we'll use a ready-made puff pastry or shortcrust.
Equally, this recipe works really well with a biscuit base of crushed digestives.

MAKES ONE 23 CM TART

500 ml (2 cups) full-cream milk
1 cinnamon stick
3 tablespoons caster sugar
3 tablespoons plain flour
1 tablespoon cornflour
pinch of salt
40 g salted butter
3 eggs, beaten

PASTRY DOUGH

50 g salted butter
225 g (1½ cups) plain flour,
   plus extra for dusting
150 ml pouring cream

TO SERVE

ground cinnamon
icing sugar

Prepare your pastry dough ahead of time. In a bowl, rub the butter into the flour with your fingers. Add the cream and mix until a dough forms. Don't over mix. Roll into a flat disc, wrap in plastic wrap and put it in the fridge to rest for about an hour.

Preheat the oven to 200°C. Grease a shallow 23 cm pie dish with butter (including the edges) and lightly flour.

In a saucepan, boil the milk and cinnamon until it just starts to bubble and rise. In a separate bowl, combine the sugar, flour, cornflour and salt. Gradually add the dry ingredients to the hot milk, stirring continuously with a whisk or wooden spoon to prevent lumps. Cook slowly, stirring continuously for 3–5 minutes, until the mixture starts to thicken. Remove from the heat and add the butter. Leave the mixture to cool for a minute or so, then very slowly stir in the eggs (you don't want scrambled eggs!).

On a lightly floured surface, roll out the pastry to a thickness of 2–3 mm and use to line the pie dish. Trim off any excess around the edges. Pour in the milk custard mix.

Bake in the oven at 200°C for 10 minutes, then reduce the heat to 160°C and bake for another 20 minutes until the tart is set. Remove and leave to cool slightly. To serve, dust with cinnamon and icing sugar and enjoy warm, at room temperature or cold from the fridge.

Samantha Hillman

WILLIAMSBURG, BROOKLYN (USA)

Samantha will be bringing

ORANGE BLOSSOM, YOGHURT AND CARDAMOM CAKE

Originally from the idyllic South Coast of NSW in Australia, Sam Hillman moved to New York as a Jill-Of-All-Food-Trades who successfully manoeuvres a career as a recipe developer, food stylist, writer and content developer.

I will never forget the first time Sam and I shared lunch. It was on one of those snowy days during the coldest February in New York for more than 80 years. As you do, she came to my house bearing a few sachets of really delicious cooking stock! As the snow fell vigorously outside, we bunkered down and cooked. I dished up a warming salad of wild mushroom and kasha (the recipe is on page 51). We chatted and laughed. By the time our bellies were full, we both looked outside and the backyard had transformed into a Narnia-esque winter wonderland. An absolutely magical afternoon, inside and out.

Sam is a throw-it-together kind of gal when it comes to baking. She is not afraid to break the rules and try new things and, in this recipe she shares with us, her bravery delivers hugely on flavour, texture and pure deliciousness.

Sam says, 'I came up with this recipe by crossing Donna Hay's yoghurt cake with a recipe for Moroccan orange blossom cake. I love to cook it for friends because it's one of those throw-it-all-in-and-give-it-a-stir type scenarios, which is perfect for me because I have the attention span of a three-year-old and refuse to let creaming butter and sugar get in the way of cake and me! I make it for anything, everything and everyone, but my favourite way to eat it is with my mum, with a pot of tea on the side.'

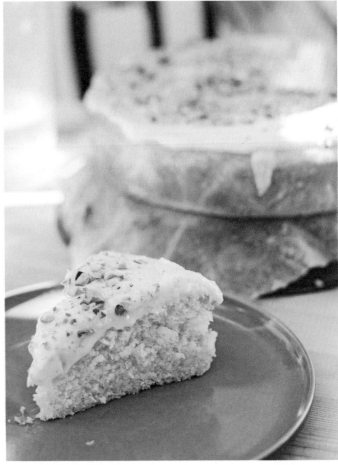

ORANGE BLOSSOM, YOGHURT AND CARDAMOM CAKE

This cake is also amazing made with macadamia oil instead of the butter! It has the same delicious taste, but stays softer for even longer.

SERVES 6-8

250 g salted butter, melted and cooled
2 eggs, beaten
2 teaspoons vanilla extract
zest of 1 orange
3 tablespoons orange juice
250 g (1 cup) Greek yoghurt
2 teaspoons orange blossom water
300 g (2 cups) self-raising flour
330 g (1½ cups) raw granulated sugar
1 teaspoon ground cardamom (or seeds
   from 8–10 cardamom pods, crushed)
2 tablespoons chopped pistachios,
   to decorate

ORANGE AND CREAM CHEESE ICING

125 g cream cheese, at room temperature
90 g (¾ cup) icing sugar
dash of vanilla extract
2 tablespoons orange juice

Preheat the oven to 160°C. Grease and line a 22 cm springform tin with baking paper.

Begin by combining the wet ingredients. Whisk together the butter, eggs, vanilla extract, orange zest, orange juice, yoghurt and orange blossom water in a bowl.

Combine the flour, sugar and cardamom and mix well.

Add the flour mixture to the wet ingredients and fold until just combined. Pour into the prepared tin and bake for 50–60 minutes, until a skewer comes out clean. Leave to cool completely.

Prepare the icing by whisking together the cream cheese, icing sugar, vanilla extract and orange juice. Combine well, until there are no lumps and the icing is smooth in texture.

Spread the icing over the cooled cake and top with the chopped pistachios. Serve immediately.

Ron and Leetal Arazi

BEDFORD-STUYVESANT, BROOKLYN (USA)

Ron and Leetal will be bringing

SHAMISHI

Soon after we arrived in Brooklyn, I received a welcome email from Ron and Leetal Arazi, then strangers to me, offering to show me around my new home borough. A few weeks later, they introduced me to the colourful, bustling Russian neighbourhood of Brighton Beach in Brooklyn. So began our food-inspired friendship.

Ron and Leetal are owners of NY Shuk, manufacturers of the tastiest Middle Eastern and North African inspired condiments. They moved to Brooklyn from Israel a few years ago, seeking to introduce New Yorkers to 'real' homemade harissa, tanzeya, l'ekama and other traditional Jewish Sephardic culinary traditions. Ron's handmade couscous is unspeakably good, while pastry chef Leetal effortlessly dishes out the most heavenly desserts.

Leetal shares her family recipe for shamishi: 'This is a cake that my grandmother made every year during our family celebration of "Tu B'Shevat", a Jewish holiday where you celebrate a "new year" for the trees. When we moved to NYC and started catering, we wanted to cook foods that authentically represent us. This is how shamishi became our signature dessert! We took the original recipe and gave it the NY Shuk treatment, reducing some of the sweetness that is typical of Middle Eastern desserts. Now, at any special dinner, shamishi cake will be served as the centrepiece. Depending on the season, we pair the cake with different toppings, from citrus fruit in the winter, to strawberry in the summer.'

SHAMISHI

This is a rose-scented semolina cake with whipped cream,
strawberry sauce and pistachios.

SERVES 80-100

875 g (7 cups) semolina
90 g (1½ cups) shredded coconut
250 g (1¼ cups) caster sugar
2 teaspoons bicarbonate of soda
½ teaspoon baking powder
pinch of sea salt
375 g unsalted butter, melted
500 g (2 cups) Greek yoghurt
100 g (¾ cup) chopped pistachios,
   to decorate

SUGAR SYRUP

1.15 kg (5 cups) caster sugar
2 tablespoons honey
juice from ¾ lemon
5 drops rosewater essence

YOGHURT WHIPPED CREAM

475 ml (2 cups) thickened cream
1 tablespoon icing sugar, plus extra
   if necessary
75 g Greek yoghurt
zest of 1 orange

STRAWBERRY SAUCE

450 g fresh or frozen hulled strawberries
1 tablespoon icing sugar, plus extra
   if necessary

IMPORTANT NOTE:

This recipe makes a HUGE shamishi cake
– and can be cut into 80–100 5 cm pieces.
Hence it is perfect for a big gathering
or party. Otherwise, to make a more
conservative amount, halve the recipe
and use a 29 x 24 cm cake tin to make
45–50 pieces. Remember to reduce the
cooking time by half if you are making
a smaller version of this recipe.

Preheat the oven to 180°C. Grease a round 46 cm cake tin or
a 46 x 33 cm baking sheet with butter.

To make the sugar syrup, place the sugar and honey in a deep
saucepan with 1.25 litres (5 cups) of water and bring to the boil
over a high heat. Make sure to mix so the sugar won't caramelise.
Once boiled, lower the heat to medium and continue cooking
until the sugar and water thickens to a syrup consistency. A
good way of testing for the perfect consistency is to put a few
plates in the freezer and place a tablespoon of the syrup on the
plate – drag your finger through it to draw a line and, if it stays,
the syrup is ready. If the line disappears then cook the syrup a
little bit more. Once ready, squeeze in the lemon juice. Leave to
cool completely, then stir through the rosewater essence and mix
together well. Set aside.

Mix the semolina, coconut, sugar, bicarbonate of soda, baking
powder and sea salt together in a bowl, add the melted better and
mix well using your hands. Once the butter is fully incorporated,
add the yoghurt and mix. Transfer the cake mixture into the
tin and use a spatula to smooth and even out the surface. Score
the cake with a knife in a cross hatch pattern to create square-
or diamond-shaped pieces that are about 5 cm in size. Bake in
the oven for 40 minutes, turning the cake around after the first
20 minutes to ensure even baking, until nice and golden. Remove
from the oven and pour over the cold syrup. Leave to cool.

For the yoghurt cream, whip the cream with the icing sugar until
soft peaks form. Gently fold in the yoghurt using a spatula, then
add the orange zest and give it one more mix. Taste and add more
sugar if you like it sweeter.

To make the strawberry sauce, using a hand-held blender, whizz
the strawberries together with the sugar until you get a smooth
sauce. Taste and add a little more sugar if you like it sweeter.

To serve, spoon 2 tablespoons of the strawberry sauce onto the
centre of a serving plate. Cut a piece of the cake and place on top,
add a dollop of the cream and sprinkle over a few pistachios.

Jodi Moreno

WEST VILLAGE AND AMAGANSETT, NEW YORK (USA)

Jodi will be bringing

RHUBARB CUSTARD TART WITH A MACADAMIA NUT CRUST AND RASPBERRY ICE

I met Jodi during the first days of spring in New York. She came to my house bearing a bag of sugar snap peas and our friendship was solidified. Jodi is wildly talented and creates mind-blowing gluten-free, dairy-free dishes. She reintroduced me to the joys of long-forgotten grains like millet and at lunch, she serves up crazy good things like horchata, a tropical Mexican drink of almond or rice milk, vanilla and cinnamon. Nowadays, when I'm looking for healthy food inspiration or just want to spoil myself by looking at pretty pictures, I often find myself digging around Jodi's beautiful blog What's Cooking Good Looking. It truly is inspiring.

Jodi has an innate ability to create healthy desserts that taste indulgent. This rhubarb custard tart is a tour de force in gluten-free and dairy-free baking – the recipe is a real eye-opener in how to achieve texture and flavour without automatically reaching for flour and butter.

For Jodi, this sweet is perfect to bring for dessert as it is healthy yet full of wonderful things such as rhubarb: 'Rhubarb is best known for being paired with strawberries and made into pie, which also happens to be the only dessert as a child I did not care for. It wasn't until I grew up and started cooking on my own that I became fascinated with rhubarb and all of the wonderful things you could make with it. Now when rhubarb comes along, I cannot get enough. These days, I am always trying to come up with desserts that are dairy- and gluten-free, but equal to or better than their butter and white flour counterparts. This rhubarb tart has become my (personal) most-loved dessert recipe because it naturally achieves that super dessert status by using ingredients that are better for you, but the best part is the vegan rhubarb custard (made possible with coconut milk and agar-agar flakes). It's so delicious, it's hard to not eat it all with a spoon before it makes its way into the tart crust.'

RHUBARB CUSTARD TART WITH
A MACADAMIA NUT CRUST AND RASPBERRY ICE

Since rhubarb is super seasonal, you can make this tart using other fruits that are in season.
Just sub in the same quantity of whatever fruit you like for the rhubarb.

VG | GF | SERVES 8

CRUST

3 tablespoons shredded coconut
200 g (1¼ cups) macadamia nuts
60 g (½ cup) rolled oats
½ teaspoon sea salt
175 g (1 cup) brown rice flour
3 tablespoons melted coconut oil
1 teaspoon vanilla extract

RHUBARB CUSTARD

7 stalks rhubarb (about 600 g), green tops
    removed and rhubarb chopped
170 ml (⅔ cup) maple syrup
¼ teaspoon ground cinnamon
1 tablespoon vanilla extract
    (or 1 vanilla pod, split and scraped)
1¼ tablespoon lime juice
¼ teaspoon salt
330 ml (1⅓ cup) coconut milk
2 tablespoons agar-agar flakes (or
    2 teaspoons agar-agar powder)
1 tablespoon orange juice

RASPBERRY ICE (OPTIONAL)

140 g (1 cup) frozen raspberries

Preheat the oven to 150°C. Grease a 23 cm tart tin.

Start by making the crust. Spread the coconut out onto a baking sheet and bake for 5 minutes until lightly toasted. Remove from the oven and tip into a food processor. Increase the oven temperature to 180°C. Add the macadamia nuts, oats and salt to the coconut in the food processor and pulse many times until you have a very finely ground texture. Transfer to a bowl and add the brown rice flour, melted coconut oil and vanilla extract and stir to form a dough. The dough should be wet and should stick together, but should not be too sticky. If it's too sticky, then leave it to sit for a few minutes to dry out slightly.

With clean hands, form the dough into a ball, then place it in the centre of the tart tin and press it in with your fingers to mould it to the tin. Poke a few holes in the bottom with a fork, then bake for 20–25 minutes until light brown. Leave the crust to cool for several minutes, then place it in the fridge to completely cool for at least an hour (you can also do this a few days in advance).

To prepare the custard, add the rhubarb, maple syrup, cinnamon, vanilla extract, 1 teaspoon of the lime juice and the salt to a heavy-based saucepan over a medium–low heat. Cook, stirring occasionally, for about 20 minutes, or until the rhubarb is very soft (if it gets too hot and starts bubbling, turn the heat down, as you don't want to burn the rhubarb). Mash the cooked rhubarb with a potato masher to a fairly smooth consistency, add the coconut milk and stir to incorporate, then stir in the agar-agar flakes and bring to a simmer. Reduce the heat to low, cover and cook, stirring every few minutes, for 15 minutes, or until the agar-agar has dissolved (just look closely to see if there are any flakes left – if there are, cook for a few minutes more). Remove from the heat and leave the mixture to cool for 10–15 minutes.

Once cooled, transfer the rhubarb mixture to a food processor, add the orange juice and the remaining 1 tablespoon of lime juice and blend for about 1 minute until the mixture is smooth. Leave the mixture to sit (in the food processor) for 10 minutes. This will allow it to cool and thicken even further. Then blend again until it's super smooth.

To assemble, pour the rhubarb mixture into the chilled tart crust and smooth the top. Place the tart in the fridge and leave to set for at least 2 hours, ideally overnight. (It's best to have patience with this one – if you cut into it too soon, the crust and the inside might fall apart. The longer it sits, the better it will hold together.)

When you're ready to serve, make the raspberry ice (this topping it totally optional). Place the frozen raspberries into the food processor and pulse several times until you have a fine-grain ice. Remove the tart from the fridge, top with the raspberry ice and serve immediately.

Charlotte Ree

GLEBE, SYDNEY (AUSTRALIA)

Charlotte will be bringing

CREAMY RICE WITH CARAMELISED PEARS

Charlotte loves food. I would almost say she lives and breathes it. When she visited me in New York, I don't think there was a moment when she didn't have an edible item in her mouth, in her hand or hidden in her bag. She loves to try it all.

While some of her encyclopaedic food knowledge may come from her day job as a book publicist talking up cookbooks, her robust food know-how actually stems from first hand experience in the kitchen. Charlotte is a baking goddess – she cooks and eats with abandon and documents these culinary feats on her wonderful blog Charlotte Eats, where she dishes up clever treats such as Bacon Brownies, Kingston Biscuits and Chocolate Peanut Butter Cheesecake. Ultimately, she owes her love of sweet indulgence to the wonderful desserts she grew up eating, including this inter-generational creamy rice recipe, which Charlotte has personalised with caramelised pears.

'My nanny gave this recipe to my mama and my mama gave it to me. We eat it warm in winter and cool in summer, a year round love hug. No matter where I am or whom I am with, making and tasting this recipe immediately transports me back to home. Memories of my nanny and mama stirring the pot on the stove or fighting my brother for the last bowlful, this is my ultimate comfort food.'

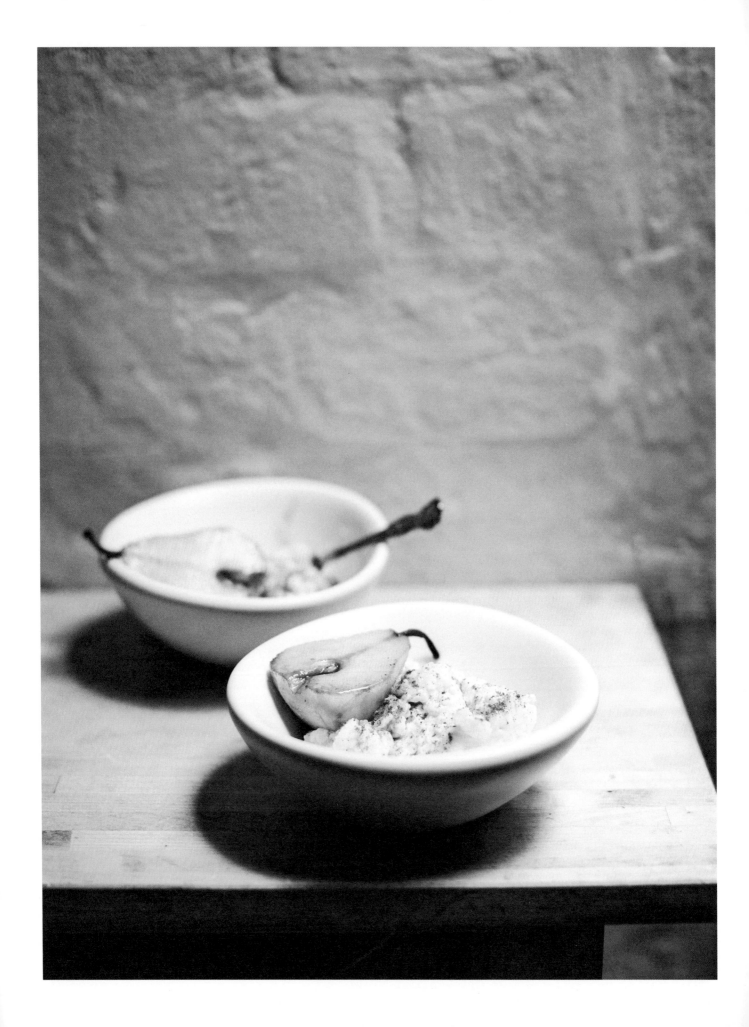

CREAMY RICE WITH CARAMELISED PEARS

Creamy rice (or rice pudding as normal folk call it) is a dessert from my childhood and my ultimate comfort food. This particular recipe has been passed down from generation to generation but I have added my own little twist to it – caramelised pears.

GF | SERVES 6, GENEROUSLY

1.5 litres (6 cups) full-cream milk
220 g (1 cup) arborio rice
115 g (½ cup) demerara sugar,
  or more depending on how much
  sweetness you prefer
1 teaspoon vanilla extract or
  1 vanilla pod, split and scraped
1 cinnamon stick
ground nutmeg, to serve

CARAMELISED PEARS

60 g unsalted butter
3 buerre bosc pears, halved
3 tablespoons soft brown sugar
1 teaspoon vanilla extract
pinch of salt

In a large saucepan, combine the milk, rice, sugar, vanilla and cinnamon. Slowly bring to the boil, stirring occasionally. Once boiled, turn the heat down to medium–low and stir constantly for 20–25 minutes until the mixture is thick and the rice grains are soft. Take off the heat.

Meanwhile, for the caramelised pears, melt the butter in a large frying pan over a medium–high heat. Add the pear pieces, cut-side down, and cook for 4–5 minutes until golden. Mix the sugar together with 1 tablespoon of water and stir to combine. Turn the pears skin-side down, add the sugar and water mixture and cook until the sauce has thickened slightly. This should take around 2 minutes. Stir in the vanilla extract and salt.

Divide the rice among serving bowls, top each with a pear half and drizzle over the caramel sauce. Sprinkle over a little nutmeg to finish.

Erika Raxworthy

HIGHBURY, LONDON (UK)

Erika will be bringing

OLIVE OIL AND SEA SALT MOLTEN BROWNIES

Erika Rax, as she is more commonly known, is a natural born creator. As is well documented on her eponymous blog, she is a home baker, compulsive crafter and freelancer, but these labels don't really even touch on the boundless talents of this girl wonder.

I first met Erika on the very first day of shooting *Community*. She offered to come help style the photographs. Not only did Erika go on to style the entire book with her signature cool aplomb (as she did with this one), she also became a good friend. Over the years, Erika and I have worked on a few projects together, but my favourite one was when she showed my daughter and her friends how to make their own terrariums. She's just handy like that. Erika is also a rabid baker, with a well-known sweet tooth. On her blog, she lays the sweet on thick with fun and clever recipes like Ginger Caramel Lava Cake, Pretzel Peanut Butter Mini Cheesecakes, Salted Caramel Swirl Marshmallows and Popsicle Affogato. Erika's perfect sharing dessert, Olive Oil and Sea Salt Molten Brownies, is a fine example of her craftiness in the kitchen:

'I found a recipe for cookies online that somewhat fit what ingredients I had in the pantry. After my adaptations, I realised that the batter was more suited to a cake. It later evolved into a brownie after I put it in the fridge and it became super fudgy.

'It's now my go-to recipe if someone is coming over or if I just need something chocolatey. I almost always use a different kind of chocolate to stir through (white chocolate or a whole hazelnut chocolate is amazing) which makes it different every time.'

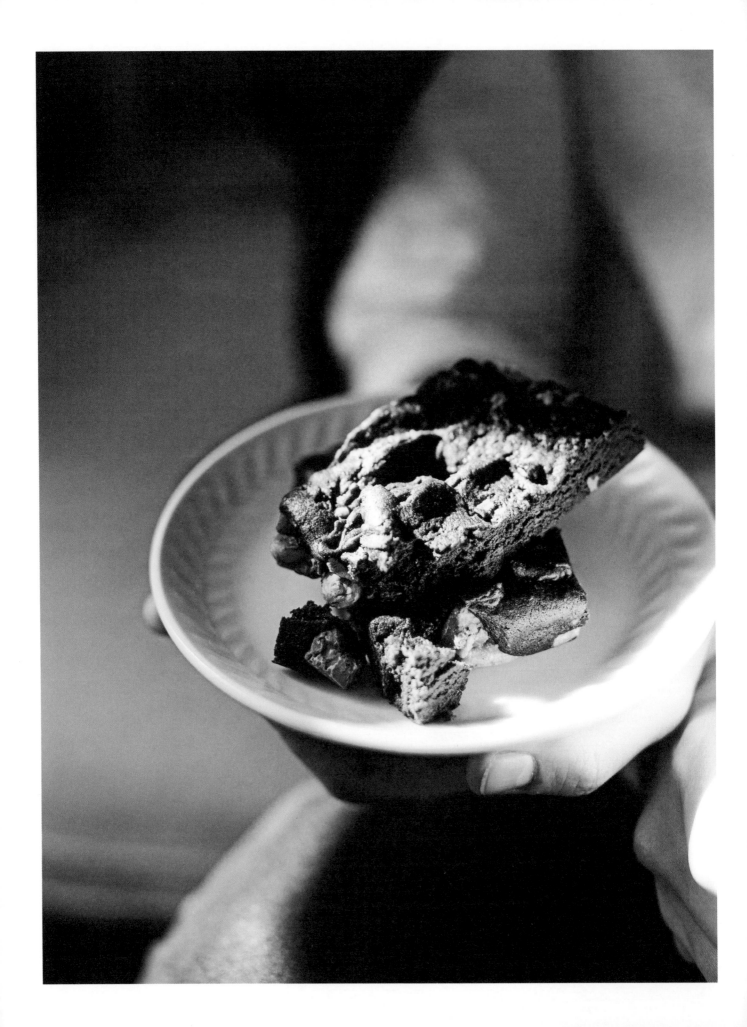

OLIVE OIL AND SEA SALT MOLTEN BROWNIES

This molten brownie is incredibly adaptable. Add in whatever half-eaten chocolate bars you have lying around in your pantry. In the brownie pictured opposite, I used a chocolate bar with peanut butter and pretzels – and it was so good!

SERVES 9-12

2 eggs
230 g (1 cup) dark brown sugar
125 ml (½ cup) extra-virgin olive oil
1 teaspoon vanilla extract
110 g (¾ cup) self-raising flour
90 g (¾ cup) cocoa powder, sifted
1 teaspoon coarse sea salt flakes
100 g chocolate, roughly chopped
   (any type will do: white, milk, dark)

Preheat the oven to 180°C. Grease and line a 22 cm square cake tin.

In a bowl, whisk together the eggs, sugar, olive oil and vanilla extract until mixed well. Add the flour, cocoa and salt and stir well to form a thick but smooth batter, then stir through the chocolate bits.

Pour the mixture into the prepared tin and bake for about 10 minutes. The centre should still be a little bit wobbly, but not liquid – poke it with your finger and if it feels set but still soft, then it's done. Don't over-bake!

Cool on a wire rack and cut into squares or rectangular slices to serve – the size of your slice is up to you! Serve slightly warm or leave in the fridge overnight and slice for super fudgy brownies. Brownies can be stored in the fridge for up to 7 days.

ACKNOWLEDGEMENTS

I began writing this book during the winter in New York City, after two months on the road in Europe, feeling inspired by family, food and life. While writing is often a solitary act, there were many people in those early snowy months in New York who provided me with friendship, who cooked with me or made me tea. Thank you to Jodi Moreno, Ron and Leetal Arazi, Wesley Verhoeve, Karen Mordechai, and Samantha Hillman for giving me an experience of writing that felt extremely social.

When I think of the people who have changed the course of my life, Luisa Brimble is at the top of that list. Thank you Luisa for being extraordinary amongst a sea of ordinary. You are a dreamer and a realist all rolled into one. There is nothing you can't achieve. Thank you once again for delivering such warmth and honesty to the images in this book. Your talent and zest for life continues to astound me.

Thank you to the third arm of our triumvirate, the incomparable Erika Raxworthy – thank you for your sharp eye and quiet determination. You are, hands down, the most creative person I know. The elegance in the way you work is matched only by your grace as a human being. I am so lucky to be on the receiving end of your immense talent.

A huge thank you to Sappho Hatzsis – the way you command the kitchen is fierce and beyond impressive. Your zen energy is very special to be around.

Huge hugs to Maria Midões, the gentle soul who takes such powerfully evocative pictures. You have such a big future, I'm just humbled to be a small part of your present. Gracias to Xochitl Adriana for your behind-the-scenes magic.

'Thank you' is simply not enough to express my gratitude to my indomitable publisher Mary Small. Every day, I have to pinch myself that I get to work with someone as inspiring and forward-thinking as you. You have guided me along my path as an author with such sensitivity, sagacity and respect – I'm so lucky to have you on my side.

Thank you also to everyone at Plum Books and Pan Macmillan Australia who all do their bit to get my books onto the shelves. Special thanks to Charlotte Ree for being a special human being – your professionalism is only surpassed by your immense heart. Thank you also to the uber-lovely Clare Marshall for your positivity and for being such a joy to work with.

Thank you to my spectacular art director Daniel New for your finesse and class. Thank you also to the meticulous Simon Davis for your dexterity with words – I think I have found someone who loves punctuation as much as I do!

Acknowledgements

Thank you to Judy Linden at Stonesong for not only keeping me on the straight and narrow, but for steering me, and this book, in the right direction. I am so grateful for your unerring belief in my story.

Thank you to all my sweet-makers scattered around the globe for sharing your friendship and sweet genius – Jennifer Wong, Charlotte Ree, Bianca Presto, Erika Raxworthy, Wesley Verhoeve, Ron and Leetal Arazi, Jodi Moreno and Samantha Hillman.

Thank you to all the booksellers of Australia who took *Community* under your wing. I wish I could meet every one of you to thank you personally. Your support of my books means so much to me.

I wanted to say a special thank you to the people of Surry Hills, where this offbeat story all began – I may be gone, but you're not forgotten.

Thank you to every person who has bought my book, given one to a friend, shared a recipe and told his or her friends about it – this grassroots support has completely humbled me. A big thank you to all those who cook my salads and then Instagram them and create hashtags like #ayearofarthurstreetkitchen (you know who you are Emma Wheater!).

Thank you to my dearest friend Davida Sweeney for your weekly phone calls from the Antipodes – your voice, your wise words and, most of all, your friendship mean the world to me.

Thank you to friends near and far who relentlessly support me on this salad adventure – Joanne Solomon, Katia Kelly, Stephen Lipuma, Amy Ng, Melanie Hansche, Jason Hoy, Matt Lennon, Dion Lee, Irma Gunadi, Lorraine Abela and Gabi Wynhausen.

Thank you to the amazing Robert Gordon family for your generosity – your plates take my salads to a whole new level of pretty! Thank you also to the amazing folk at Staub, Brooklyn Slate and Utopia Goods.

Thank you to my family: my mother Lindy who raised us with the smell of ginger on her hands, and wonderful food on the table every night. Thank you to my big sister Letty and big brother Kerby for keeping things real.

My heart belongs to my little peeps – Scout, Dash and Huck – after all these years, I still can't choose which one of you is my favourite, so you'll have to settle for sharing the title. Thank you for agreeing to eat the salads I dish up so regularly, and with smiles on your faces too!

This book is dedicated to my husband. This salad commotion couldn't happen without him at my side. Simply, he is so rad.

~HM

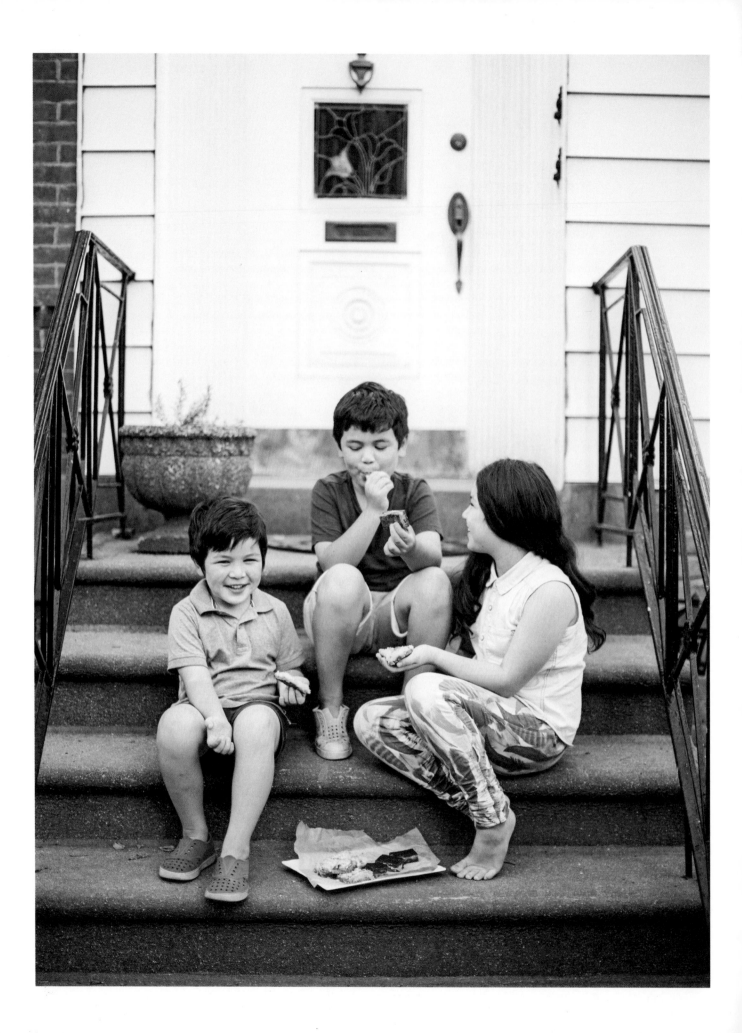

INDEX

A Plum book

First published in 2016 by

Pan Macmillan Australia Pty Limited

Level 25, 1 Market Street,

Sydney, NSW 2000, Australia

Level 1, 15–19 Claremont Street,

South Yarra, Victoria 3141, Australia

Design by Daniel New

Edited by Simon Davis

Index by Hannah Koelmeyer, Tusk Studio

Photography by Luisa Brimble (with additional photography by Erika Raxworthy and Maria Midões)

Prop and food styling by Erika Raxworthy

Food preparation by Sappho Hatzsis and Hetty McKinnon

Typeset by Kirby Jones

Colour reproduction by Splitting Image Colour Studio

Printed and bound in China by 1010 Printing International Limited

The publisher would like to thank the following for their generosity in providing props for the book:
Robert Gordon Australia, Staub, Utopia Goods and Zwilling J.A. Henckels.

1 3 5 7 9 10 8 6 4 2